From Abraham to Armageddon

End times revealed through Israel

Dr. Harold Michael Phillips

Contents

Acknowledgments

Introduction

Sixteen Questions That Need Answers

Question #1

Did God reveal His plan before the Jewish people were called for His special purpose?

Question #2

Who are these people called the chosen people of God?

Question #3

Why are Isaac's descendants called the chosen people of God?

QUESTION #4

Does God have a long-term plan for the people called the Jews? If so, what is it?

QUESTION #5

What about the seed of the other child of Abraham, Ishmael?

QUESTION #6

What happens when God's chosen people reject God for the gods of the world?

QUESTION #7

Will God be angry at Israel forever?

QUESTION #8

What happened to the people of God when they rejected God's only begotten Son?

QUESTION #9

Why do the Gentiles now claim to be a part of God's chosen people? Is this biblically accurate?

QUESTION #10

How did this kingdom, preached by John the Baptist and Jesus, become a part of this plan? Was it a new concept?

QUESTION #11

How did the Church become part of God's plan for His world? How does the Church fit into the kingdom, and with the chosen people?

QUESTION #12

What happens to the Jews during the Church age?

QUESTION #13

How does the Church age come to a close?

QUESTION #14

What is Armageddon?

QUESTION #15

What happens after Armageddon?

QUESTION #16

What then?

CONCLUSION

How it applies to us

ENDORSEMENTS

"May I recommend this book with great enthusiasm? It is instructive and challenging, and will greatly bless the Christian who desires to know more of God's word, God's works, and God's way. I trust you'll read it as soon as possible."

Dr. Bailey E. Smith, Evangelist
Bailey Smith Ministries
Atlanta, GA
Former President of the Southern Baptist Convention

"Dr. Phillips has given us a unique approach to the study of the end times. Tracing the subject from Abraham to Armageddon is fresh and helpful. You will enjoy the book."

Dr. Jerry Vines, Pastor
First Baptist Church of Jacksonville
Jacksonville, FL
Former President of the Southern Baptist Convention

ACKNOWLEDGMENTS

I would like to say a deep thanks to my family for their continued patience during the time I was involved in studying and writing this book. There were many days that I was found in deep study when I was needed by them. I appreciate their love and understanding. Thank you, Joshua, Chad, Caleb, Luke and Kristen. I especially want to thank my wife for her encouragement over the years. Thank you, Corkie, my best friend.

I thank Pleasant View Baptist Church, in Port Deposit, Maryland, for the inspiration to continue in labor for Christ. I thank all the members for their inspiration and encouragement. I would also say a hearty thanks to Bear Springs Baptist Church in Dover, Tennessee; Sylvia Baptist Church in Dickson, Tennessee; Eunity Baptist Church in Cheraw, South Carolina; Trace Creek Baptist Church in Mayfield, Kentucky; Flat Rock Baptist Church in Anderson, South Carolina; and Friendship Baptist Church in Honea Path, South Carolina for their love, patience and investment in my Christian growth.

I also would like to thank my parents, Billy Ray and Annie Ruth Phillips, my brothers, Brian, Steve and David Phillips, and my sister, Cathy Kennedy for their love and encouragement. Thanks so much for being there.

There are many, many others I would love to name, but the list would be too long. Therefore, thanks to all who have encouraged and invested in me over the years. God bless you, everyone. You know who you are.

INTRODUCTION

Israel – God's Grand Billboard

Israel – God's Public Timepeace

Israel – God's Revealing of Himself to Man

Israel – Truth Outside of Me

This book is one person's observation as to how God answers the many who have asked the questions:

- **Is there a God?**
- **If so, does He have a reason for creating the people called the Jews?**
- **Is He manipulating the events of the world to serve His purpose?**
- **To what extent has He already determined what has taken place and will take place in this world?**

In the fall of 1977, I was a young man who had just surrendered to the ministry. A relative of mine asked me a question that I could not answer. "What about this nation Israel? What have they to do with the end times and the coming of the end of the world?" At the time I was unable to answer that question. I have been searching for the answer ever since. I believe that I have found the answer and have written it down.

Jimmy, this book is for you!

It is my intention to help the reader understand that God is the ultimate authority of the universe. God is using the nation of Israel as a tool to proclaim His existence as well as His personality. Israel is God's billboard, God's timepiece, and God's ultimate focus of revelation. Through them He has declared His existence, His plans for the future, His control of the future, His righteousness, and His expectation of righteousness from those in good standing with Him. Through His people, He has revealed the fact that He will judge unrighteousness and reward righteousness. Through them, He has given us the answers to our questions. Where did I come from? Who am I? What is wrong with me? What do I need to do to be right with Him? Who is He? What does the future hold? When will all these things come to pass? And yet He provides so much more. I hope you can understand the importance of studying the Bible and the nation of Israel. A study of the Bible and the nation of Israel will unlock the past, present and future. A study of the Bible and the nation of Israel will help us find purpose in this misled and confused world.

It is my intention to help the reader understand that God has established absolute truths. There are truths outside of us. In this day of postmodernism, it is hard to find people who believe in absolute truth. Everything has become subject to questions. We who believe are looked on as "out of touch with reality," when actually the opposite is true. If we do not discover that there are truths beyond us, we are likened to a captain trying to navigate a vessel across the ocean without anything to guide us but a lantern on the front of the boat. But there are still other issues we must concern ourselves with. We do not even know where we are trying to navigate to. Remember the questions being asked:

- **Is there a God?**
- **If so, does He have a reason for creating the people called the Jews?**
- **Is He manipulating the events of the world to serve His purpose?**
- **To what extent has He already determined what has taken place and will take place in this world?**

I would like to address these issues by answering sixteen questions about God and the Jews.

QUESTION # 1

Did God reveal His plan before the Jewish people were called for His special purposes?

The answer is yes! Let me illustrate:

Before Abraham

After the dispersing of Noah's ancestry at the tower of Babel, God established the lineage of Shem in the scriptures. Genesis 11:10-32 gives the description of the ancestors of Abraham. Abraham was of the lineage of Shem and was, therefore, one of the children of Noah who were to be blessed. Genesis 9:26-27 tells us *"And he said, Blessed by the LORD God of Shem; and Canaan shall be his servant. God shall enlarge Japheth, and he shall dwell in the tents of Shem; and Canaan shall be his servant."*

Abraham was in the favor of God because Shem was in the favor of God. Because of this, God chose the nation of Israel to be a blessing for the world. He chose a man named Abram. But this was not the first event that happened in the scriptures. There were other truths to be learned. Let us examine a few of these very valuable lessons together.

It is a fact that there were verses and chapters in the Bible before the mention of Abraham, but there were not many

– there were only 295 verses. Abram's promises became the focus of attention throughout the Bible beginning in Genesis 11:29. The rest of the Bible seems to be driven by what God said to Abram. In Genesis 12:1-2 we find *"Now the LORD had said unto Abram, Get thee out of thy country, and from thy kindred, and from thy father's house, unto a land that I will shew thee: And I will make of thee a great nation, and I will bless thee, and make thy name great; and thou shalt be a blessing:"*

But even before Abram there were many important lessons taught. Let's briefly discuss a few of these lessons and then we will return to the focus of Abraham and his children.

God's Family Plan (Adam and Eve)

It is not hard to find God's plan for the family in the very first pages of the Bible. It is also easy to understand that God's plan was for one man to find a special woman. That woman was designed for him by God, and he was to minister to her and join with her in order to raise a family that would walk with and honor God. The family was the first relationship between God and man. Men and women were to link together and labor together. Adam's loneliness was the compelling reason for the creation of woman. Woman was created for the purpose of companionship and support in the life of man. The very first thing God said was that it was not good for man to be alone, and then He stated He would make a helpmate. Therefore, woman was created to end man's loneliness and to give him a helping hand with life. God has a plan for life that is distinct and complete. Anyone looking for the truth of the purposes and goals for the family will not need to look far to find the facts. God does have a plan for the family.

God's Testing Plan (Serpent in the Garden)

It is important to note that God established an examination in the Garden of Eden a few verses before Adam was given his bride. The tree of the knowledge of good and evil found in chapter three of Genesis was not put there for Eve only. It is clear it was there in order to test both of God's created humans. But what was the test all about? On a test there is always some type of question. The question can come in various forms: true or false, fill in the blank, or a discussion question. But this time the question was being asked of Adam and Eve every time they walked by the tree, "Do you believe in God?"

God clearly informed Adam in Genesis 2:16-17 *"And the LORD God commanded the man, saying, Of every tree of the garden thou mayest freely eat: But of the tree of the knowledge of good and evil, thou shalt not eat of it: for in the day that thou eatest thereof thou shalt surely die."*

First, let's understand the basic principle here. This was a command, not a suggestion. This also was a warning – straight and to the point. If you eat of this tree, you shall surely die. The command was given to provide them a way of testing themselves as to what they believed. This test was to see if Adam and Eve trusted God's word. If they believed what God had said, they would surely have stayed away from this tree. But it is clear that the serpent established a few questions that compelled Eve to need to find out if God was telling the truth. The test seems to be whether or not Eve believed God. Why would this be so important? You see, God *is* truth. It is part of His being, and if He is not truth, then He is not God (and the ultimate good). Truth and trust were the real test questions. Therefore, when the Philippian jailer asked in Acts 16:30 *"...Sirs, what must I do to be saved?"* Paul replied in verse 31, *"...Believe on the Lord Jesus Christ, and thou shalt be saved, and thy house."* It could be assumed that the statement "and thy house" was there to note that Adam lost his house when he and Eve chose not to believe. Therefore, when the jailer chose to believe, he would be reinstated with God, and he would take his house back to God. It is important that we see on the first pages of the written message from God how He establishes the foundation of the relationship between God and man – believing God.

And what about the statement made by God, "thou shalt surely die?" There is no question; God said, "Thou shalt die." Did Adam and Eve die? When we define death as physical death, we must say no. They did not die (nor do we for a few years), but the death that God was referring to was a different kind of death – the death that comes with a separation from God. God is life, and when we are away from Him we die, just as when we leave light we automatically receive darkness, because darkness is the absence of light. Death is separation from God. Adam and Eve could no longer walk in the presence of God, could not look into His face. From that point on in the Bible, we learn that man was sent out of the Garden and away from God. From that day until the coming of Jesus incarnated in flesh, we would not be able to be in the presence of God. This puts a whole new picture to becoming a born-again Christian. When we become a part of Christ, we believe that we are reconciled to God. Now death has no power over us, because Jesus promised that He would never leave us nor forsake us. Therefore, when we are reconciled to Christ, we are reinstated with God and eternal life. We are, as Paul told the Corinthians, "reconciled to God." 2 Corinthians 5:17-19 tells us, *"Therefore if any man be in Christ, he is a new creature: old things are passed away; behold, all things are become new. And all things are of God, who hath reconciled us to himself by Jesus Christ, and hath given to us the ministry of reconciliation; To wit, that God was in Christ, reconciling the world unto himself, not imputing their trespasses unto them; and hath committed unto us the word of reconciliation."*

The test is now ours. We must decide if we believe the Word of God, which declares His Son. If we believe on Him, we shall be saved. Thus, we return to the presence of God. This helps us understand the indwelling of the Holy Spirit as well as the other references to the indwelling presence of God. It helps us see why the Holy Spirit could not come to us until the death, burial and resurrection. It helps us see why the Spirit does not come to us until we believe. This also gives new meaning to the words of Jesus in John 11:25-26, when He told Martha, whose brother had died, *"I am the resurrection and the life: he that believeth in me, though he were dead, yet shall he live: And whosoever liveth and believeth in me, shall never die. Believest thou this?"* Until I understood the Genesis principle of death, I had a hard time understanding what Jesus meant by these words. And so, in the words of Jesus, the Christ, "Believeth thou this?"

God's Worship Plan (Cain and Abel)

Cain and Abel – what is the valuable lesson God is trying to teach us with these two brothers and their struggle? Note: this is after the fall of man and the exit from the Garden. It seems man is trying to find a way to come before God and be looked on favorably.

In Genesis 4:1-5 we find:

> *"And Adam knew Eve his wife; and she conceived, and bare Cain, and said, I have gotten a man from the Lord. And she again bare his brother Abel. And Abel was a keeper of sheep, but Cain was a tiller of the ground. And in the process of time, it came to pass, that Cain brought of the fruit of the ground an offering unto the LORD. And Abel, he also brought of the firstlings of his flock and of the fat thereof. And the LORD had respect unto Abel and to his offering: But unto Cain and to his offering he had not respect. And Cain was very wroth, and his countenance fell."*

It is clear that these two brothers were trying to find a way for God to accept them back into His favor. Cain's failure is a lesson we all must grasp. Cain tried to get into the favor of God by his own homegrown offering. It is clear that an offering needs to be presented to God in order for man to please Him. It seems when we give God something valuable as a gift, we are saying that He is more important to us than the gift. Able discovered the way to get into the good graces of God. He trusted on the work of another to get him back to God. He trusted on the work of a lamb in order to gain the respect of and favor with God. Therefore, we learn on the first pages of Genesis, before Abraham, that something must die in order for us to be brought back into the flock of God. A sacrifice must be given. And so, we see many offering sacrifices to God – animal sacrifices. I must point out here that the lamb, of course, represented the coming Christ who, as John the Baptist said, would take away the sins of the world.

It is also clear that God was trying to help us see that there are only two ways man tries to get back to God – the Cain way of human effort, or the Abel way of trusting on the Lamb of God. Of course, the only way to please God, as we have learned here, is the way of the Lamb.

Every religion in the world is either trying to please God by works, or they are truly pleasing God by trusting on the finished work of Jesus.

How are you trying to be reinstated to God – the way of Cain or Abel?

God's Worship Plan (Cain and Abel)

It is becoming clear that God already knew what He would do to help man unite with Him again. In Genesis, 10 righteous men in the genealogy from Adam to Noah stood out in their service to the Lord. If you list their names in order, it declares God's ultimate plan to visit mankind. He knew He would be treated harshly while visiting, but in turn, He would be able to purchase great rewards for His followers. The greatest reward is the reinstitution of the man/God relationship.

Let me show you what I mean. These Hebrew names recorded in Genesis 5:4-29 have very important meanings. When the names and their meanings are put together, the message is amazing!

- Adam – Man
- Seth – Appointed
- Enos – Mortal
- Cainan – End
- Mahalaleel – Mighty God
- Jared – To Come Down
- Enoch – A Mortal
- Methuselah – At His Death Judgment Will Come
- Lamech – Sorrow
- Noah – Comfort Us

Man is appointed to a mortal end. The mighty God is to come down a mortal man and, at His death, judgment will come with sorrow, but He will comfort us.

This is truly a proclamation of the awesome God we serve!

Even before the flood, God knew He needed to come down as a man and die as a man in order for man to be comforted.

Yes, He did come down a mortal man, and yes, He does comfort men.

Is He comforting you?

God's Frustration Plan (Noah's Ark)

The story of the flood is without question a proclamation that God will judge the sins of man. It also teaches us that God brings sweeping judgment on the world when the preaching of the Word does not affect the hearts of men to repent of their sins and return to righteousness and a proper relationship with Him. It seems to frustrate God when mankind is wicked in his heart and will not heed the proclamation of truth. When man rejects God's counsel, God has no alternative but to reject man and issue judgments that will establish an example for those who follow.

When God can no longer break through the sin-calloused heart of man (for He will not force Himself on anyone), God has no alternative but to act with swift and powerful judgments. But for those who will repent and believe God, He will protect, provide for, take interest in, and raise the believer above the judgment coming to unbelievers.

Are you one of the believers or one of the unbelievers?

Man's Disaster Plan (Tower of Babel)

In Genesis chapter 11, man decided to invest his energies into building a tower toward the sky, clearly indicating that man had a hard time focusing on service to God. This tower is a direct proclamation of disobedience and a statement to God that they did not need Him.

Genesis 11:4 confirms this statement: *"And they said, Go to, let us build us a city and a tower, whose top may reach unto heaven; and let us make us a name, lest we be scattered abroad upon the face of the whole earth."*

They felt they could reach to Heaven, if only they could stay together and work as a unit. But God's direction to Noah and his seed was to go forth and populate and replenish the Earth. They did not want to be scattered abroad, so they disobeyed God and gave the impression that they did not need Him. It was then that God divided them by bringing confusion to their communication. This caused them to scatter abroad, therefore we inherited an Earth divided, segregated and in conflict.

This chapter gives us knowledge as to where the different countries and races of people came from, and how they became divided. But Christ, in the Great Commission, tells us now to go and unite to work together to build a Church that will reach around the world and into the heavens.

Christ is now constructing a building that will reach the real Heaven. He is doing so by calling all of us to become united now into one fellowship. We are called to proselytize the world into one unit under one language – the language of love. He is using language now to unite, just as He once used language to divide. This is what the Day of Pentecost is all about. Acts 1 and 2 establish the beginning of the unification of one Church reaching for Heaven, only this time with God's help and blessing. This is a reversal of Genesis 11, because now God is uniting the people. He is breaking down those confusing barriers commissioning a mission into the entire world and uniting all races into one body, directing all who will cooperate to Heaven by and through Jesus Christ.

Acts 1:4-9 tells us:

> *"And, being assembled together with them, commanded them that they should not depart from Jerusalem, but wait for the promise of the Father, which, saith he, ye have heard of me. For John truly baptized with water; but ye shall be baptized with the Holy Ghost not many days hence. When they therefore were come together, they asked of him, saying, Lord, wilt thou at this time restore again the kingdom to Israel? And he said unto them, It is not for you to know the times or the seasons, which the Father hath put in his own power. But ye shall receive power, after that the Holy Ghost is come upon you: and ye shall be witnesses unto me both in Jerusalem, and in all Judea, and in Samaria, and unto the uttermost part of the earth. And when he had spoken these things, while they beheld, he was taken up; and a cloud received him out of their sight."*

In Acts 2:1-12 we find:

> *And when the day of Pentecost was fully come, they were all with one accord in one place. And suddenly there came a sound from heaven as of a rushing mighty wind, and it filled all the house where they were sitting. And there appeared unto them cloven tongues like as of fire, and it sat upon each of them. And they were all filled with the Holy Ghost, and began to speak with other tongues, as the Spirit gave them utterance. And there were dwelling at Jerusalem Jews, devout men, out of every nation under heaven. Now when this was noised abroad, the multitude came together, and*

were confounded, because that every man heard them speak in his own language. And they were all amazed and marvelled, saying one to another, Behold, are not all these which speak Galileans? And how hear we every man in our own tongue, wherein we were born? Parthians, and Medes, and Elamites, and the dwellers in Mesopotamia, and in Judaea, and Cappadocia, in Pontus, and Asia, Phrygia, and Pamphylia, in Egypt, and in the parts of Libya about Cyrene, and strangers of Rome, Jews and proselytes, Cretes and Arabians, we do hear them speak in our tongues the wonderful works of God. And they were all amazed, and were in doubt, saying one to another, What meaneth this?

We look to Genesis and Acts for the formation and the commissioning of mankind. One must understand the book of Acts and the coming of the Holy Spirit and the reason for the gift of languages. It is important to note that in Genesis, at the tower of Babel, the people were confounded by their lack of ability to understand each other's' language. Therefore, when God gave the language blessing in Acts 2, it was not to confuse but to give help, direction, and understanding of God's plan. Those in the large crowd from other countries heard the Galileans speak to them in their own languages. This gift of tongues was not a confusion of voices as some have led us to believe. It was not to be an unknown angelic language or a super communication with God. This was a coming together of the sons of Noah by restoring their ability to communicate with each other.

It is all a part of a very detailed plan of God. The time has come, however, with God's help, to bring everyone back into unity. Now is the time to reach toward Heaven. But now this time with God's blessing and with God's help. We can now reach Heaven only after the cleansing and reinstatement to God has taken place. This finally was made possible by the death of the Lamb of God, Jesus Christ.

God is calling a group of workers to go and be used by Him to help mankind understand and come into a relationship that brings man back to Him. John 14:1-3 confirms this as follows: *"Let not your heart be troubled: ye believe in God, believe also in me. In my Father's house are many mansions: if it were not so, I would have told you. I go to prepare a place for you. And if I go and prepare a place for you, I will come again, and receive you unto myself; that where I am, there ye may be also."*

God is putting together a work force!

Are you a part of this work force?

God has a plan:

- God has a plan for the family!
- God has a plan for worship!
- God has a plan of rescue!
- God has a plan for judgment!
- God has a plan to reach Heaven!

This is what is in the first five major stories of the Bible. Then He calls Abraham and proceeds to carry out His plans.

QUESTION # 2

Who are these people called the chosen people of God?

The names and what they mean

It is important to note that God changed Abram's name to Abraham in Genesis chapter 17. He renewed the covenant with him and gave Abram a way to mark himself and his future sons. That mark was circumcision. It was a private act between parents and their children.

Abram means "exalted father," and Abraham means "father of a multitude." This name change was God's way of reminding Abraham of his future blessings. Every time Abraham's name was called (by anyone), Abraham was reminded of his future and the impact he would command.

Jews

The Israelites were first called Jews in Esther 2:5-6 *"Now in Shushan the palace there was a certain Jew, whose name was Mordecai, the son of Jair, the son of Shimei, the son of Kish, a Benjamite; Who had been carried away from Jerusalem with the captivity which had been carried away with Jeconiah king of Judah, whom Nebuchadnezzar the king of Babylon had carried away."*

The meaning of the word Jew is derived from a Hebrew word meaning "celebrated find" or "celebrity." It is where we get our word for "jewel" – some say the Jews are called the joy (celebration) of God; **Jew**, meaning "to celebrate," and **el**, representing God. Hence – jewel. This word originated and is derived from the place of their dwelling, Judea or Judah, which means "a people cast forth in celebration of who they are."

So when God made the Jews, He found a reason to celebrate. When the people of God discovered God and His interest in them, they had a reason to celebrate.

Israel

The word Israel was first mentioned in Genesis 32:28. We are reminded, *"And he said, Thy name shall be called no more Jacob, but Israel: for as a prince hast thou power with God and with men, and has prevailed."* Jacob, being the grandson of Abraham and knowing the promises, had an extreme desire to have these promises fulfilled in his life. He tried to make them come to pass by unrighteous means –lying and deceiving. But now God was changing his life. God, in changing his life, changed his name, and his purpose as well. Jacob was asking God to bless him, but the only way God would bless Jacob was for him to change his ways (New Testament picture of repentance). Therefore, God changed his purpose as He changed Jacob's name to Israel. The word Israel is derived from two Hebrew words – **Isra** (power of a prince) and **El** (almighty or strong like God). Thus – we obtain the meaning of "Prince of God."

Hence, when one finds God changing him from selfishness to servanthood, one must change one's purpose and become a child of God. Romans 8:15-16 tells us *"For ye have not received the spirit of bondage again to fear; but ye have received the Spirit of adoption, whereby we cry, Abba, Father. The Spirit itself beareth witness with our spirit, that we are the children of God."*

Hebrews

The people of God were first called Hebrews in Genesis 14:13 *"And there came one that had escaped, and told Abram the Hebrew; for he dwelt in the plain of Mamre, the Amorite, brother of Eshcol, and brother of Aner: and these were confederate with Abram."* They were called Hebrews because they were descendants of Eber. We find this in Genesis 10:21 – *"Unto Shem also, the father of all the children of Eber, the brother of Japheth the elder, even to him were children born."* Eber was one of the sons of Shem. (Shem is thought to be the firstborn son of Noah, because of the repetitious order of the three sons listed – Shem, Ham and Japheth – Genesis 5:32; 6:10; 9:18, etc.).

Note: Eber had two sons called Peleg and Joktan. Peleg was born during an earthquake. He was named after this earthquake, which brought great separations when it happened. Hence, Peleg and his children would be the separated in days to come.

Joktan means "he will be made small." It seems his name typified his life, for we do not know much about him or his descendants. However, Peleg's name and his descendants made up for the deficiencies of his brother.

Abraham and his children were descendants of Eber, who birthed Peleg (earthquake or one who divides). Abraham was a descendant of Peleg the divider. It became clear that the children of Abraham would bring the chief divisions to the Earth. Because of the Hebrews and God's promises to them, a major division became present on the Earth. It seems God was giving us a hint as to the division that would be brought upon the earth by Abraham's calling (since he was the great grandson of Peleg, the divider, as recorded in Genesis 11). It is amazing that, after the call of Abraham, there was a division in the Earth. The world would experience a two-part system after Abraham's call. Now there would be Jews (Hebrews) and the other people, called Gentiles. Abraham's call was the "earthquake" that divided the whole human race. Therefore, throughout the Old Testament, any time the word "Hebrew" or "Jew" was used, the division was apparent.

God did not hide the fact that He had chosen Abraham. The rest of the world would be outside of that favored status. That would last until Jesus came. Now we are told in Acts 10 that God sent Simon Peter to Cornelius' house. Cornelius, a Roman (Gentile), was invited by Peter to become part of the chosen ones. In Romans 9:24-25, Paul writes, *"... whom he [God] hath called, not of the Jews only, but also of the Gentiles? As he saith also in Osee, I will call them my people, which were not my people; and her beloved, which was not beloved."*

Jesus Himself gave the marching orders to the disciples in Matthew 28:18-20. There He told them to go to all the world and make disciples, and He said this to Jewish disciples. The verse that everyone knows, John 3:16, *"For God so loved the world, that he gave his only begotten Son, that whosoever believeth in him should not perish, but have everlasting life,"* was said to a Jewish

Pharisee! The old, the young, the rich and the poor, the Jew and the Gentile – all were invited! Did you get that? He invited the whole world – ALL the whosoevers!

This was real news – real and wonderful news. God has used the Jews to distinguish Himself in the world. He used the Jews to declare Himself to the world, and now He will use them to bring salvation to the whole world. Now God only sees two groups of people: believers in Christ and non-believers, saved and not yet saved, followers of Christ and lost ones.

John 7:40-43 identifies this when it states, *"Many of the people therefore, when they heard this saying, said, Of a truth this is the Prophet. Others said, This is the Christ. But some said, Shall Christ come out of Galilee? Hath not the Scripture said, That Christ cometh of the seed of David, and out of the town of Bethlehem, where David was? So there was a division among the people because of him."*

Jesus Himself tells us in Matthew 10:32-39:

> *Whosoever therefore shall confess me before men, him will I confess also before my Father which is in heaven. Think not that I am come to send peace on earth: I came not to send peace, but a sword. For I am come to set a man at variance against his father, and daughter against her mother, and the daughter in law against her mother in law. And a man's foes shall be they of his own household. He that loveth father or mother more than me is not worthy of me: and he that loveth son or daughter more than me is not worthy of me. And he that*

> *taketh not his cross and followeth after me, is not worthy of me.*

The New Testament illustrates this in the following passages:

Acts 14:3-7:

> *Long time therefore abode they speaking boldly in the Lord, which gave testimony unto the word of his grace, and granted signs and wonders to be done by their hands. But the multitude of the city was divided: and part held with the Jews, and part with the apostles. And when there was an assault made both of the Gentiles, and also of the Jews with their rulers, to use them despitefully, and to stone them, They were aware of it, and fled unto Lystra and Derbe, cities of Lycaonia, and unto the region that lieth round about: And there they preached the gospel.*

Acts 23:7

> *And when he had so said, there arose a dissension between the Pharisees and Sadducees: and the multitude was divided.*

The final separation is demonstrated as follows:

Matthew 25:31-34, 41

> *When the Son of man shall come in his glory, and all the holy angels with him, then shall he sit upon*

> *the throne of his glory: Any before him shall be gathered all nations: and he shall separate them one from another, as a shepherd divideth his sheep from the goats: And he shall set the sheep on his right hand, but the goats on the left. Then shall the King say unto them on his right hand, come, ye blessed of my Father, inherit the kingdom prepared for you from the foundation of the world: Then shall he say also unto them on the left hand, Depart from me, ye cursed into everlasting fire, prepared for the devil and his angels:*

Eber and Peleg's children divide. The only question is: which side will you take?

It is a deep study to look into the names that the God of the Bible establishes with the Old Testament people. God was saying much more with their names than simply pointing out an individual.

The people of God were chosen to establish a race of people that would be called "God's people," and they would divide the world into two categories. Eventually, through their descendant, Jesus Christ, they will divide eternity for all of us. It is no secret God has chosen the people of Abraham to divide, and with that division many will be rejecters of God. But many will become the "jewels" of God. This seems to be God's ultimate eternal goal – to find jewels. Are you one of God's jewels?

One might realize that there was a division before Abraham. Remember Cain and Abel and the division brought about by the differences in their worship for their Creator? The problem wasn't whether or not God existed, nor was it that Cain did not please God. The problem was that Cain wasn't willing to humble himself and ask God what he needed to do to please Him. Instead he became upset and killed his brother. Many have criticized the element of worship as being divisive and causing wars, and worldwide problems. However, honest men might admit the problem is not the worship of God. It is quite clear that the problem is in the pride-filled hearts of man. It is important to note that division over worship will exist, but in reality there are only two religions in the world – Cain's way of works or Abel's way of grace. There is no disputing this fact. That is simply the way it is.

Gentiles

The Gentiles are the other people who are first mentioned in Genesis 10:5. This verse tells us, *"By these were the isles of the Gentiles divided in their lands; every one after his tongue, after their families, in their nations"*

The Gentiles were divided from the Jews, but they would also be divided among themselves. The word Gentile comes from the word **"goy,"** which is the same as **"gevah,"** (the people in the back, or the people behind). "Goy" refers to the masses or foreign nations. Hence, Gentiles were people left out of God's chosen few. The illustration used to describe the word "goy" is a group of animals or a flight of locusts. It denotes those simply going through the world, taking without compassion or laws, except for the law of selfish motivation. They exist as animals without the ability to know God. This is why animals today are left out of the ability to know God. "Goy," or Gentiles were left out of that circle, and left only to be motivated by the laws of selfish motivation: food, feelings, and reproduction. Therefore, being a Gentile meant that they were not a part of the Jews (celebration of God). They were not able to be Israel (princes of God), and they were separated from God.

The Word of God is such a rich and insightful book. A simple word study on the names used for the chosen people and the word Gentile tells us so much about God's plan. The main thing it tells us is that God is in charge, and that God is offering us the chance to become His chosen princes and princesses.

Before we become too frustrated at the fact that God chose one people over another people in the past, we must understand that He used His chosen ones to offer sonship to mankind. We must also point out that becoming the chosen people brought great pain upon the Jews from all around the world. But now we all are given the opportunity to be His celebrated ones (His princes and princesses), but we are also His dividers as well.

This gives new meaning to the words in Ephesians 2:11-22.

> *Wherefore remember, that ye being in time past Gentiles in the flesh, who are called Uncircumcision by that which is called the Circumcision in the flesh made by hands; That at that time ye were without Christ, being aliens from commonwealth of Israel, and strangers from the covenants of promise, having no hope, and without God in the world: But now in Christ Jesus ye who sometimes were far off are made nigh by the blood*

> *of Christ. For he is our peace, who hath made both one, and hath broken down the middle wall of partition between us; Having abolished in his flesh the enmity, even the law of commandments contained in ordinances for to make in himself of twain one new man, so making peace; And that he might reconcile both unto God in one body by the cross, having slain the enmity thereby: And came and preached peace to you which were afar off, and to them that were nigh. For through him we both have access by one Spirit unto the Father. Now therefore ye are no more strangers and foreigners, but fellow citizens with the saints, and of the household of God; And are built upon the foundation of the apostles and prophets, Jesus Christ himself being the chief corner stone; In whom all the building fitly framed together growth unto an holy temple in the Lord: In whom ye also are builded together for an habitation of God through the Spirit.*

It also gives new meaning to the words of Jesus in John 15:18-19, *"If the world hate you, ye know that it hated me before it hated you. If ye were of the world, the world would love his own: but because ye are not of the world, but I have chosen you out of the world, therefore the world hateth you."*

Conclusion: when the facts are in, God is God, and He is control. God is now offering to all an invitation to become chosen, and anyone who becomes one of the chosen ones will have a lot to celebrate. But, one can also expect to be separated from all other beings, especially those living a selfish existence, as defined in the word Gentile.

This gives new meaning to many passages, especially 1 Peter 2:9 where we find, *"But ye are a chosen generation, a royal priesthood, an holy nation, a peculiar people, that ye should shew forth the praises of him who hath called you out of darkness into his marvelous light:"*

What will you do?

QUESTION # 3

Why are Isaac's descendants called the chosen people of God?

Genesis 12:1-3

> *Now the LORD had said unto Abram, Get thee out of thy country, and from thy kindred, and from thy father's house, unto a land that I will shew thee: And I will make of thee a great nation, and I will bless thee, and make thy name great; and thou shalt be a blessing. And I will bless them that bless thee, and curse him that curseth thee: and in thee shall all families of the earth be blessed.*

The call of Abraham was the beginning of the nation of Israel and the beginning of the proclamation of God's plan. I am sure Abraham did not know just how much his life and calling would affect the world. He left home in search of a land that God would show him. He never saw the earthly land of Israel that we know today. He did walk on the land, and by his faith in God, he knew that it would eventually be the homeland of his future family. According to Genesis 12:5-7, Abraham knew which land would be his children's, even though he never saw them possess it with earthly eyes. *"And Abram took Sarai his wife, and Lot his brother's son, and all their substance that they had gathered, and the souls that they had gotten in Haran; and they went forth to go into the land of Canaan; and into the land of Canaan they came. And*

Abram passed through the land unto the place of Sichem, unto the plain of Moreh. And the Canaanite was then in the land. And the Lord appeared unto Abram, and said, Unto thy seed will I give this land: and there builded he an altar unto the LORD, who appeared unto him."

Promised Blessing

By the Genesis proclamation, God has promised to bless Abraham and his seed. Also, God has promised to bless anyone who would bless Abraham's seed, and to curse anyone who curses the seed of Abraham. The following passages confirm this:

Genesis 12:1-2

> *Now the LORD had said unto Abram, Get thee out of thy country, and from thy kindred, and from thy father's house, unto a land that I will shew thee: And I will make of thee a great nation, and I will bless thee, and make thy name great; and thou shalt be a blessing.*

Genesis 17:6

> *And I will make thee exceeding fruitful, and I will make nations of thee, and kings shall come out of thee. And I will establish my covenant between me and thee and thy seed after thee in their generations for an everlasting covenant to be a God unto thee, and to thy seed after thee, And I will give unto thee, and to thy seed after thee; the land wherein thou art a stranger, all the land of Canaan, for an everlasting possession; and I will be there God.*

Promised to Bless

God also promised that He would use the nation of Israel, and that it would be formed to be a blessing to all other nations. How could this be possible? God birthed His only begotten Son out of the family of Abraham and, through His Son's sacrifice, offered salvation to the world.

Genesis 12:3

> *And I will bless them that bless thee, and curse him that curseth thee: and in thee shall all families of the earth be blessed.*

Israel Possesses Their Promised Land (From Promise to Possession)

God kept the promises that He made to Abraham and his children. He did so, even though He sometimes used unpleasant circumstances to bring about His will (like putting them in Egypt, as a result of a famine). He then left them in the land for over four hundred years. They ended up there as a result of brotherly jealously, but God used it as a means to keep His promises to the children of Abraham:

Joseph's troubled ways (Genesis 37 – 46)

It is hard to understand from a worldly viewpoint why God allowed many of these things, but from a spiritual perspective, we can see the reasoning.

The two sons of Isaac, with their jealousy, seemed to initiate this (Genesis 27). Then the selfish struggles of the twelve sons of Jacob compounded the problem. They all ended up in Egypt under the brother they had mistreated.

What a story! It seems that God is not only using the nation of Israel to fulfill His eternal plans; He is also using their struggles to teach us many practical lessons.

I want to give a brief summary of the Jewish experience of taking possession of the Promised Land. I want to share it as if you have never heard it. I do this because there will be people who read this book who have never experienced this. I encourage all to open the Bible and read of this amazing move of God. It is an exciting story!

The process of heading toward the Promised Land started when Joseph was sold into slavery by his brothers. He spent practically his whole life in Egypt, sometimes as a slave, sometimes as a prisoner, and eventually as the second highest ruler in the kingdom. Only God could have arranged such a drama. Then because of a famine, Jacob (Joseph's father) moved the whole family to Egypt. God works in strange ways.

They seemed to be extremely blessed while in Egypt. They were so blessed by God that the Egyptians became afraid of them and began to persecute them. They eventually enslaved them and, by the beginning of the book of Exodus, the Egyptians were trying to kill all the Jewish male children for fear they would eventually take over Egypt. Then God raised up a man named Moses to deliver them from the land of Egypt.

After over 400 years in Egypt, God brought them out in His power, under the leadership of Moses. The book of Exodus tells this amazing story. God sent plague after plague until finally, the oldest child of every household that did not kill a lamb and mark the doorpost with its blood was killed. Then the Egyptians drove the Israelites out of Egypt.

Moses left Egypt with millions of God's chosen. The children of Abraham went into the wilderness, headed for the Promised Land. They were unaware of where they were. Moses just knew that God told him to bring them to a specific mountain for further instructions.

It is important to note that God was leading Moses across the desert, and He brought them to the Red Sea where there was no place to go. Pharaoh then decided he did not want to let them go without retaliating for the death of his son and the children of Egypt, so he went after them.

God held Pharaoh back with a pillar of fire and then parted the Red Sea so the children of Israel could cross on dry land. Pharaoh followed them into the sea and he and his soldiers were killed when the walls of water collapsed on them. The Exodus experience was not over after they crossed the Red Sea; it had only just begun.

They had to trust God for every meal, every drink of water, every day of protection. God then gave them the gift of the Law. Until this time, the children of Abraham were running on traditional rights and wrongs handed down by their parents. Then the Law came. It started with the Ten Commandments and grew to a whole series of guidelines. These guidelines were not complete until the coming of Jesus. He came to fulfill the Law.

God brought them to the Promised Land. They had a time of weak faith and refused to cross the Jordan River into the land of Canaan. This refusal sent them into the wilderness for forty years of wandering. They wandered around for forty years until the generation that did not have faith enough to go where God was leading them had perished.

Moses also died and did not go into the land because he had been disobedient. Their children went into the land under the leadership of Joshua and Caleb, two of Moses' generals. The book of Joshua tells the story of their entrance into the land, their battles, and the blessings that God placed upon them resulting from their faith.

The creation, sustenance, protection, and leading of a the blessed children of Abraham were all miracles from God. It took faith on the part of the children of Abraham to come out of Egypt and cross the Red Sea into the wilderness. It took faith to endure the wilderness experience. Those who did not believe paid dearly for their disbelief. They did not get the privilege of being a part of the group that entered the Promised Land.

It takes a strong faith for you and me to believe the things that God has said He has done to deliver His people. Faith is, of course, the key for them (and us). They did conquer the Promised Land, and the markers are there to prove it. It cost them greatly when they did not believe God. Now God has called on us to believe the report. It will cost us greatly if we do not.

Yes, the Jews were in the land of promise. God kept the promise made to Abraham, but there were many promises yet to be fulfilled. Faith and a continual walk with God were needed to see that those other promises would be fulfilled.

The point is, however, God chose to give the Promised Land to the child of Sarah, who was Isaac. This is a major issue today in the Holy Land. They fight daily over who has the right to call this land of promise theirs. According to the record of the Old Testament writers, Moses and his people were given the land of promise. Remember, Moses is a descendent of Isaac, which grants him that right from God's Word.

Why are they called the promised seed? Because God promised they would be, and that they would be blessed!

But remember the ultimate questions:

- **Is there a God?**
- **If so, does He have a reason for creating the people called the Jews?**
- **Is He manipulating the events of the world to serve His purpose?**
- **To what extent has He already determined what has taken place and will take place in this world?**

QUESTION # 4

Does God have a long-term plan for the people called the Jews? If so, what is it?

When reading the Bible we learn that, from Genesis 12 to Revelation 22, the children of Abraham are at the center of God's plan for man and his eternal life. God calls on one man and his descendants to bless the world with the declaration of what is righteous (the Law of Moses). He declares the importance of the sacrificial lamb, the power of the lamb's blood, and the importance of service to Him above all else. He heralds the coming of the King who will eventually rule the world from the city in the center of the world, Jerusalem (place of peace). God uses Abraham's children. He created a people who are often small in physical stature and often disliked. They are the worldwide underdogs. They have been disliked and mistreated by the majority of people as long as they have existed. This gave them the greatest amount of time on the world's stage, and that is an important thing in our day of world news. This center-stage position has established a focus on Abraham and Armageddon that will proclaim worldwide the truth about a coming appointment with the God of the universe. The Bible continually declares that there is coming a day of war when all nations will meet in the valley of Megiddo to end life on Earth as we know it.

Abraham is called the father of three major religions – Judaism, Christianity and Islam.

It is God's biblically declared intention to create a nation that will be blessed by God but hated by the world. This combination may seem to lack understanding, but is causes a great deal of attention to be placed on Israel. However, it also creates a great interest in biblical knowledge as well as biblical prophecies.

I would like to discuss a special story about two people from the Bible that will help us realize God's intention for the children of Abraham. This story gives us a brief picture of the plans established by God. It is the story of Hosea and Gomer, which is found in the Old Testament of the Bible and is in the middle of a section called the minor prophets.

The name Hosea (salvation) comes from the root word for salve (ointment). We also get our word salvage from this root word. Therefore, it implies that God needs to salvage something. The nation of Israel is what needs to be salved (anointed) or salvaged (saved). Why do they need to be salvaged? They have moved away from God and are in the sinful service of the gods of this world. Hosea is a faithful prophet who is told by God to marry a harlot. He then goes out and marries a women who is practicing harlotry with many lovers. He brings her home and tries to make a respectable woman out of her. He loves her even with her sinful past. There is little known about Hosea other than that he was a prophet of Israel from 770-725 B.C. He prophesied during the time when the nation of Israel was split into two countries, Northern Israel and Sothern Judea. He prophesied beginning in 2 Kings 14:23-27.

During most of Hosea's lifetime, the people of God were spiritually bankrupt. Their leaders permitted them to practice idolatry (2 Kings 15:35) and to commit spiritual "harlotry" against the Lord (Hosea 2; 4:15). They refused to recognize that God had provided them with wealth and prosperity (Hosea 2:8). In fact, they attributed their prosperity to their idols (Hosea 2:5; 10:1). Despite the calls for punishment from God, they continued to reject Him for other gods. Hosea, in his obedience, went and took a wife from this whoredom and he raised children of whoredom. Hosea married a woman named Gomer, the daughter of Diblaim. The name Gomer means complete. It seems we are being told that the meaning of the union between Hosea (salvation) and Gomer (complete) is that she will bring completion to his life in the same way Eve brought completion to the life of Adam in the creation story. But because Hosea's name means salvation, which comes from the root word for salve (ointment), it seems his name is implying that Gomer needs some medicine to be well. She needs to be salvaged. Isn't this interesting?

Hosea married Gomer, the harlot. He brought her home and made her a well-respected wife and mother. She conceived and bore him a son, Jezreel. She also bore two other children from her harlot lifestyle whom Hosea seems to have treated as his own. However, no matter how Hosea tried, Gomer would not forsake her other lovers. She continued to go to them and reject her good, godly, loving husband. Hosea even sent the three children to plead with their mother to come home, but she refused.

Finally, Hosea could not bear to have his heart broken any longer. He couldn't' get Gomer to forsake her lovers, so he left her to whoredom. She would not stop, so Hosea let her go and simply prayed that God would put a hedge of protection around her. Many years passed, and Gomer spent herself in rejection of Hosea, following other lovers until she was old, defeated, broken and bruised. One day

Hosea came through town and saw his Gomer being sold as a slave, but no one seemed to want her. Hosea not only bought her, but also paid a high price for her. He purchased her and brought her back to their home. He reinstated her as his wife again. This time she would forsake the lovers of the past. This time she was glad to be home.

Notice Hosea 4:1. God tells Israel that their problem is that they have no truth, mercy, or knowledge of God. Hosea declares that when truth, mercy and knowledge are absent from your situation, there will be lying, killing, stealing, adultery, and blood touching blood. And yes, there can be no question that is what Hosea and Gomer had.

Hosea and Gomer are a declaration of God's earthly plan for the nation of Israel. God created a word picture for us with the lives of Hosea and Gomer. Hosea is the picture of God and Gomer is the nation of Israel in bondage to other lovers. God married her in harlotry and made her a respectable, wealthy, well-dressed and well-blessed bride. But, after a short honeymoon, Israel just could not stay with her husband. Although He loved her selflessly and had accepted her the way she was, Israel continually ran away serving other gods and other lovers, continually giving herself to them. God took her back time after time, even trying to get her children to beg her to come back to God, but all to no avail. Israel continued to run away, all the while attributing her wealth and blessings to other gods.

Remember in the days of Moses – while Moses was on the mountain getting the Ten Commandments, God's chosen people were attributing their deliverance to the golden calf they had just created.

Finally, God simply let Israel go to her other gods and gave up trying to keep her with Him. But, as we know from many passages, God will again call her back to His house and into His protective custody, just as Hosea did Gomer.

I hope you can see the word picture created by Hosea and Gomer and identify it with the future of Israel.

If the story of Hosea and Gomer is the declared word picture of the future, at what stage is the nation of Israel now? God has declared His plans for Israel in the story of Hosea and Gomer, as well as in many pages of prophecies from both the Old and New Testaments. God has also clearly tried to convey His plans to His followers, but has concealed His plans from others in such a way that even the devil cannot discover them. However, to those who would hunger to know Him and His will, He has chosen to reveal His truth, but only in His time.

As God declares His intentions and His plans for Israel and the world, and we discover the truths found in those intentions and how they fit into present activities, we become confident in God.

Another wonderful declaration of God's plan comes in the form of the Seven Jewish Feasts celebrated annually. They are given in the Old Testament book of Leviticus, chapter 23. God gave them a yearly reminder of what He had done and what He was going to do. These were Jewish holidays that reminded them of their past rescue from Egypt and their future gathering with the King sent from God. Let's discuss them.

In order to give you a look at these feasts through the eyes of a great dispensational writer from the beginning of the 1900s, I would like to insert an account of these feasts given by Clarence Larken. You will notice that Mr. Larkin continues to talk about the regathering of the Jews and only by faith could he see this happening. Of course, the Jews did not begin to regather until after 1947. Therefore, it is amazing to see these feasts from his perspective.

Seven Feasts of the LORD

The 23rd chapter of the Book of Leviticus gives us an account of the "Seven Great Feasts" of the LORD. They were a prophecy and foreshadowing of future events, part of which have been fulfilled, and part are yet to be. They are the "shadow of things to come," of which Christ is the "body" or substance. Col. 2:16, 17. They were "Holy Convocations" of the people. They were instituted by the Lord. The people had no voice in the matter. God promised that if the males went up at the "set time" to Jerusalem to keep these Feasts, He would look after their families. When the people became formal and indifferent, the Lord said, "Your new moons and your appointed Feasts My soul Hateth; they are a Trouble unto Me; I am weary to bear them." Isaiah 1:14. Therefore Jesus called them the "Feasts of the Jews," rather than the "Feasts of the Lord."

The "Feasts of the Lord" are seven in number. If we include the Sabbath there are eight. But the Sabbath stands by itself. It was to be observed "weekly," the other Feasts "annually." The Sabbath was to be observed at "home," the other Feasts at "Jerusalem."

The "Seven Feasts" may be divided into two sections of "four" and "three." The first section includes the "Passover," the Feasts of "Unleavened Bread," of "First Fruits" and "Pentecost." Then there was an interval of four months, followed by the Feasts of "Trumpets," Day *of Atonement," and "Tabernacles." The "Three Great Festivals" were the "Passover," "Pentecost," and "Tabernacles." They extended from the 14th day to the 22nd day of the Seventh Month.*

The First Four Feasts foreshadow truths connected with this present Gospel Dispensation and those who form the "heavenly" people of the Lord, the Church; while the Last Three Feasts foreshadow the blessings in store for God's "earthly" people, the Jews.

1. The Passover Feast

   The Passover Feast had its origin in Egypt. It was the memorial of the redemption and deliverance of the Children of Israel from Egypt. It was to them the "beginning of months," and their birthday as a Nation. Exodus 12:2 It consisted of the taking of a male lamb, without blemish, of the first year, a lamb for a family, and killing it on the 14th day of the month in the evening, and sprinkling its blood with a bunch of hyssop on the two side posts and upper lintel of the door of their houses, so that when the Lord passed through Egypt that night and saw the blood on the doorposts, He would spare the first-born sheltered within. The flesh of the lam was to be roasted, and eaten with unleavened bread and bitter herbs, and none of it left until the morning. Those who ate of it were to do so with their loins girded, their shoes on their feet, and their staff in their hand, ready to leave Egypt.

   The Passover Feast was to be to them as a "Memorial," and they were to keep it as a Feast throughout their generations, and as an ordinance forever. Ex 12:14.

The Passover Lamb was intended as a "type" of Jesus, the

"Lamb of God."

The shedding of His blood on Calvary and our applying it to our hearts by faith has the same effect as to our salvation as the applying of the Passover Lamb's blood to the doorposts of those Egyptian houses had to the safety of those who were sheltered within. As that night was the "beginning of months" to them, so the moment a soul accepts Jesus Christ as Saviour, that moment it is "born again," and a new life begins, for Christ Our Passover was sacrificed for us. 1 Cor. 5:7.

The first time the Children of Israel observed the Passover Feast it was amid the terrors of God's judgment plagues in the land of Egypt, a type of the world. Thereafter, its yearly observance was as a joyful Memorial of their deliverance from Egypt. While they still observe the Passover Feast no lamb is slain, and no "blood" used, but when they get back to their own land, they will again keep the Passover. The Christian Church does not observe the Passover, but they do observe, as a Memorial, the ordinance of the Lord's Supper that Christ instituted in its place.

2. *The Feast of Unleavened Bread*

The Feast of Unleavened Bread began on the day after the Passover, and continued for seven days. Lev. 23:6-8. The lamb was slain on the 14th day at sunset, which ended the day. The Feast of Unleavened Bread began immediately after sunset, which was the beginning of the 15th day. Thus, there was no interval between them. As the Passover is a type of the death of Christ, so the

Feast of Unleavened Bread is a type of the "Walk" of the Believer, and there should be no interval between the salvation of a soul and its entrance on a holy life and walk. The "seven days" point to the whole course of the Believer's life after conversion.

Leaven in the Scripture is a type of evil, so the Feast was to be kept with "unleavened" bread. Ex. 13:7. Paul speaks of "malice" and "wickedness" as leaven. "Purge out therefore the 'old leaven' that ye may be a 'new lump,' as ye are unleavened. For even Christ our Passover is sacrificed for us. Therefore let us keep the Feast, not with 'old leaven,' neither with the 'leaven of malice and wickedness,' but with the 'unleavened bread of sincerity and truth.'" 1 Cor. 5:7-8.

The typical teaching then of the Feast of Unleavened Bread is that, having been saved by the blood of Christ our Passover, we are to "walk" in newness of life, purging out the leaven of worldliness, and doing no "servile work," or work that is done to earn salvation.

3. The Feast of First-Fruits

The Passover took place on the 14th day of the month, the Feast of Unleavened Bread on the next day, which was the Sabbath, and the following day, which was the "morrow after the Sabbath," the Feast of First Fruits was to be celebrated. This however could not be done until after the Children of Israel had entered Canaan, therefore, the Feast of First Fruits was not observed during the Wilderness Wanderings. The Offering was a sheaf reaped from the waving fields of the ripened harvest, and carried to the priest to be waved before the Lord for acceptance, and was to be followed by a Burnt, Meat and Drink-Offering, but no Sin-Offering.*

The Burnt-Offering was to be a male lamb without blemish of the first year.

The Feast of the First-Fruits was a type and showing of the

Resurrection of Christ.

He arose on the "morning after the Sabbath," and His resurrection is spoken of by Paul as the "First-Fruits" of the resurrection of the dead. As the "Corn of Wheat." (John 12:24). He was buried in Joseph's Tomb, and His resurrection was the "First-Fruits" of the Harvest of those who will be Christ's at His coming. 1 Cor. 15:23.

When the Priest on the day of Christ's resurrection waved the sheaf of "First-Fruits" in the Temple, it was before a "rent veil," and was but an empty form, for the Substance had come and the shadow had passed away, and the empty tomb of Joseph proclaimed that the "Great First-Fruits' Sheaf" had been reaped and waved in the Heavenly Temple. There will be no Feast of First Fruits in the Millenium, it has been fulfilled in Christ.

4. *The Feast of Pentecost*

   Fifty days after the Feast of First-Fruits, the Feast of Pentecost was observed. The space between the two feasts, which included Seven Sabbaths, was called the "Feast of Weeks." It began with the offering of the First-Fruits of the Barley Harvest, and ended with the ingathering of the Wheat Harvest. The First Day was the Feast of the First-Fruits; the last day was the Feast of Pentecost. Only the First and Last day were celebrated (..).

At the Feast of Pentecost, a New Meat Offering was to be offered before the Lord. It was called "new" because it must be of grain from the new harvest. At the Feast of First-Fruits "stalks of grain" were to be offered and waved, but at the Feast of Pentecost the grain was to be ground and made into flour, from which two loaves were to be baked with leaven. The "two loaves" represent the two classes of people that were to form the Church, the Jews and Gentiles, and as believers are not perfect, even though saved, that imperfection is represented by the leaven.

A "Burnt Offering" of seven lambs without blemish of the first year, one young bullock, and two rams, was to be offered with the "Wave Loaves," as was also "Meat" and "Drink" Offerings for a sweet savor unto the Lord. These were to be followed by a "Sin Offering" of a kid of the goats, and two lambs of the first year for a "Peace Offering." The "Wave Loaves" were to be waved before the Lord. Note that it is now "loaves," not loose stalks of grain. The "loaves" represent the homogeneousness of the Church.

The Feast of Pentecost had its fulfillment on the Day of Pentecost, when the disciples of the Lord were baptized into one body by the Holy Spirit. 1 Cor. 12:3.

The Interval

Between the Feast of Pentecost and the Feast of Trumpets there was an interval of four months during which the Harvest and Vintage were gathered in. There was no convocation of the people during those busy months. This long "Interval" typifies the "Present Dispensation" in which the Holy Spirit is gathering out the elect of the Church, and during which Israel is scattered among the Nations. When the present dispensation has run its course, and the "Fullness of the Gentiles" has been gathered in (Rom. 11:25) along with the "remnant according to the election of grace" of Israel (Rom. 11:5), then this "Dispensation of Grace" will end, and the elect of Israel will be gathered from the four quarters of the earth to keep the Feast of Trumpets at Jerusalem. Matt. 24:31.

5. The Feast of Trumpets

The Feast of Trumpets, which was observed on the first day of the Seventh month, ushered in the second series of the "set feasts." It fell on a Sabbath day, at the time of the New Moon, and ushered in the Jewish New Year. It was followed by the "Day of Atonement" on the 10th day of the month, and by the "Feast of Tabernacles" which began on the 15th day of the month, a Sabbath day, and ended on the 22nd day of the month, which was also a Sabbath day. It was ushered in with the blowing of trumpets. During the Wilderness Wandering two silver Trumpets, made of the anointment money of the people, were blown for the "calling of the Assembly," and for the journeyings of the Camps." Num. 10:1-10.

The fact that the Feast of Trumpets comes immediately at the close of the "Interval" between the two series of "set feasts" is not without significance. As we have seen the "Interval" represents this "Dispensation of Grace," and we know that two things are to happen at the close of this Dispensation. First, the Church is to be caught out, and secondly Israel is to be gathered back to their own land. When the Church is caught out--"The Lord Himself shall descend from Heaven with a shout, with the voice of the Archangel, and with the Trump of God" (I Thess. 4:16), and "We shall not all sleep (die), but we (who are then alive) shall all be changed in a moment, in the twinkling of an eye, at the

Last Trump;

for the Trumpet shall sound, and the dead shall be raised incorruptible, and we shall be changed" 1 Cor. 15:51-52.

This "last trump" is not the last of the "Seven Trumpets" that sound in the Book of Revelation, for it does not sound until the "Middle of the Week," while the Church is caught out "before" the beginning of the "Week." We probably are to understand by the "last trump" the last of the Two Trumpets used by Israel, the first, for the "calling of the Assembly," will call out the dead in Christ from their graves, and the second or "last," for the "journeying of the camps," will be the signal for the upward journey of the risen and transformed saints to meet the Lord in the air.

Then we read in Matthew 24:31 that the Son of Man, when He comes in the clouds of heaven with power and great glory at His revelation of Himself, shall send His angels with a great sound of a Trumpet, and they shall gather together His "elect" (not of the Church but of Israel) from the four winds, from one end of heaven to the other." From this we see that the "Feast of Trumpets" has a typical relation to the "catching out" of the Church, and the regathering of Israel at the Second Coming of Christ. This has led some to believe that as Jesus was crucified at the time of the Passover, and the Holy Spirit was given at Pentecost, that when He comes back, the "Rapture" will take place at the Feast of Tabernacles, and the "Revelation" seven years later at the time of the same Feast. Time alone will reveal the correctness of this view.

6. *The Day of Atonement*

   The "Day of Atonement" was Israel's annual cleansing from sin. For a full account of the day and its services read Lev. 16:1-34. Its typical meaning was fulfilled in Christ. He is our Great High Priest, who instead of offering a "Sin Offering" for Himself, offered Himself as a "Sin Offering" for us. Hebrews 9:11-14. But the fact that the "Day of Atonement" is placed between the "Feast of Trumpets" which we have seen will have its typical fulfillment at the Second Coming of Christ, and the "Feast of Tabernacles," which is a type of Israel's "Millennial Rest," implies that it has some typical significance between those two events. It must therefore refer to the time when a "Fountain will be opened to the

   ## House of David

   and to the inhabitants of Jerusalem for sin and for uncleanness." Zech. 13:1. That is, there will be a National "Day of Atonement" for Israel after they have been gathered back to their own land unconverted, and shall repent and turn to God. Zech. 12:9-14.

7. *The Feast of Tabernacles*

   This was the last of the Seven Set Feasts. It was a "Harvest Home" celebration to be observed at the end of the harvest, and was to continue seven days. Deut. 16:13. The people during the Feast were to dwell in booths (arbors) made of the branches of palm trees and willows from the brook, which would remind them of the palm tree of Elim, and the "Willows" of Babylon. Ps. 137:1-9. The Antitype of this Feast has not as yet appeared, though Peter anticipated it, when on the Mt. of Transfiguration he said--"Lord, it is good for us to be here; if thou wilt, let us make here three Tabernacles; one for Thee, and one for Moses and one for Elias." Matt. 17:4. What Peter desired, the swelling of heavenly with earthly people on the earth, was not possible then, but will come to pass in the Millennial Days, when Heaven and Earth shall in be closer union. The Feast of Tabernacles points forward to Israel's "Millennial Rest."

What the "Seventh Day," or Sabbath, is to the week, a day of rest;, so the "Seventh Month" is to the other six months of the "Seven Month Cycle," typifies a period of rest—the

"Sabbatical Rest"

of the "Millennial Age," or 1000 years, in relation to the other six thousand years of the world's work day history. Like the Lord's Supper is to us, a "Memorial" pointing back to the "Cross" and forward to the "Coming," so the "Feast of Tabernacles" will be a "Memorial" to Israel, pointing back to Egypt and forward to Millennial Rest.

While the Feast of Tabernacles began on the Sabbath and continued seven days, it was to be followed by a Sabbath. Lev. 23:39. This Sabbath on the "Eighth Day" points to the New Heaven and Earth that follow the Millennium, and to the "Eighth Dispensation," the Dispensation of the "Fulness of Times (...)"[1]

Yes, these feasts are amazing events from a history (His story) point of view. A summary of these feasts, and their meanings will give us an idea of what God has done, is doing, and is going to do.

1. **Feast of Passover**: This celebration declared God's protection of the Jews in Egypt, because they had faith enough to place lamb's blood over the door post of their house. God sent the death angel to kill the oldest child in every home in Egypt that was missing the blood. This was the last plague in a series of plagues in Egypt as Moses, by God's power, delivered them from slavery to go to the land promised to Abraham's seed. The Jewish people celebrated this feast as the New Year feast each year in the spring. This feast also declared the need for the blood to shelter us from the death angel. Jesus became the Lamb and shed His blood to protect us from death.
2. **Feast of Unleavened Bread**: This feast declared the pure, undefiled life required to walk with God after deliverance. This feast also declared that the sinless Son of God would come into the world to die for the sins of the world.
3. **Feast of First Fruits**: This feast was a picture of the need for us to give God our first fruits. God gave us His first and only begotten Son, and this Son became the first to conquer death. He was and is the first Resurrected One. They celebrated this feast to remind them and us that God deserves our first fruits.
4. **Feast of Pentecost**: This feast was the celebration that began the harvest season. They celebrated this feast as the harvest began. The people of Israel celebrated by waving loaves of leavened bread in the air before God. This typified the joining of the Jews and the Gentiles together. The

leaven was a symbol of sin and how the sinners of the world were now to be harvested. The harvest was plainly declared in Acts 2 of the New Testament when the writer says, *"When the day of Pentecost was fully come..."* This signified the time of year but also signified the time on God's calendar. It was harvest time. This was a long celebration.

5. **Feast of Trumpets**: This feast was the beginning of the gathering of the Jews for a time of union with God. They would go forth at the end of harvest time blowing the trumpet and gathering the Jews from the fields to end the harvest. This is a celebration of thanksgiving for the harvest.

6. **Feast of Atonement**: This feast historically was the foundation for Zechariah 13:1, and was made possible by Calvary. But to the Jews it was a time for the nation to be cleansed. They would have the priest sacrifice a lamb for the nation and cleanse the whole nation for God's use.

7. **Feast of Tabernacles**: This feast is the period of time when the Jews would gather together around their capital city, which became Jerusalem. They would come together and gather up sticks to build temporary shelters. This was a type of vacation for the Jews. They would do no work, but just celebrate being the chosen of God. They would live in these stick houses, which some believe typifies their temporary stay here on this planet.

These feasts celebrated the past deliverance of the Jewish people, but they are much more than that. These feasts also celebrate the future of the Jews as well as the rest of the world. Remember, when we started this study, we said that we believe the Jews are God's timepiece, through

God's Word and plan. We should know what time we are in. When examining the feasts, one must think of them in the same light.

The Feast of Passover was declaring the deliverance from death by the lamb in Egypt. This feast was of great importance, because it declared the coming of the Lamb who would die to protect us from the death angel. John 11:25-26 says, *"... I am the resurrection and life: he that believeth in me, though he were dead, yet shall he live: and whosoever liveth and believeth in me shall never die. Believest thou this?"*

The Feast of Unleavened Bread declared not only the need for the Jews to be pure, but the need for the Gentiles to be pure as well.

The Feast of First Fruits declared their need to give God their best, but we also need to give God our best. We owe God this because He has given us His best. It is that fruit of Jesus that became the first fruit to come up from the ground.

The Feast of Pentecost was the beginning of the harvest for the Jews. It is certain that God also marked this as the beginning of His earthly harvest, meaning it is part of the Day of Pentecost as well. We find this in Acts chapter 2, where the harvest began as the Church age began.

The Feast of Trumpets ended the harvest of the Jews agriculturally. There will be another trumpet which will end the harvest of God from the fields of this world (1 Thessalonians 4:13-18). There can be no question that, when the trumpet sounds, the Pentecost harvest time will be over, and the gathering will begin. God will gather His Church from the four corners of the Earth. And God will finish gathering His unsaved Jews from the four corners of the globe.

The Feast of Atonement marked the Jewish gathering to purify their nation before God. And the seven years of tribulation called "The Day of Jacob's Trouble" will also purge the nation of Israel for the Feast of Tabernacles.

The Feast of Tabernacles was the time when the Jews would go to Jerusalem to celebrate God and their relationship to Him. It will be the same in the future Millennial Reign of Christ. This is the one-thousand-year rule of the King of the world. All this will come to pass in the future as the Millennial Reign of Christ.

I hope you can see the dual purpose of the seven feasts. It is important to note that the first three have already happened. We are living in the Pentecost/Church/Harvest day now. The next three will be the trumpet for the rapture, the finished regathering of the Jews, and their time of purging. After that the one thousand years of tabernacle celebration will finally occur.

If all this is true, what time is it now? It is Pentecost time, the time for the world to be harvested. What will end Pentecost time? The trumpet blast!

Past:

- Passover – Jews
- Unleavened Bread – Jews
- First Fruits – Jews

Present:

- Pentecost – World Harvest

Future:

- Trumpets – Jews
- Atonement – Jews
- Tabernacle – Jews and Gentiles

Now let me ask you:

- **Is there a God?**
- **If so, does He have a reason for creating the people called the Jews?**
- **Is He manipulating the events of the world to serve His purpose?**
- **To what extent has He already determined what has taken place and will take place in this world?**

Yes, God has declared that His King will eventually rule the world from the throne of Jerusalem. Let's examine that part of God's plan. Zechariah 14:1-9 says:

> *Behold, the day of the LORD cometh, and thy spoil shall be divided in the midst of thee. For I will gather all nations against Jerusalem to battle; and the city shall be taken, and the houses rifled, and the women ravished; and half of the city shall go forth into captivity, and the residue of the people shall not be cut off from the city. Then shall the LORD go forth, and fight against those nations, as when he fought in the day of battle. And his feet shall stand in that day upon the mount of Olives, which is before Jerusalem on the east, and the mount of Olives shall cleave in the midst thereof toward the east and toward the west, and there shall be a very great valley; and half of the mountain shall remove toward the north, and half*

> *of it toward the south. And ye shall flee to the valley of the mountains; for the valley of the mountains shall reach unto Azal; yea, ye shall flee, like as ye fled from before the earthquake in the days of Uzziah king of Judah: and the LORD my God shall come, and all the saints with thee. And it shall come to pass in that day, that the light shall not be clear, nor dark: But is shall be one day which shall be known to the LORD, not day, nor night: but it shall come to pass, that at evening time it shall be light. And it shall be in that day that living waters shall go out from Jerusalem; half of them toward the former sea, and half of them toward the hinder sea: in summer and in winter shall it be. And the LORD shall be king over all the earth: in that day shall there be one LORD, and his name one.*

Jesus declared in His own words that He will be that King and that His followers will be there with Him and assist Him. Will you be in that group? Matthew 25:31-34 says, *"When the Son of man shall come in his glory, and all the holy angels with him, then shall he sit upon the throne of his glory: And before him shall be gathered all nations: and he shall separate them one from another, as a shepherd divideth his sheep from the goats: and he shall set the sheep on his right hand, but the goats on the left. Then shall the King say unto them on his right hand, Come ye blessed of my Father, inherit the kingdom prepared for you from the foundation of the world."*

The Apostle Paul declares this truth in 1 Corinthians 6:2, *"Do ye not know that the saints shall judge the world? And if the world shall be judged by you, are ye unworthy to judge the smallest matters?"*

QUESTION # 5

What about the seed of other child of Abraham, Ishmael?

Problem child (Ishmael)

Although it is indeed sad, there was a child that was not wanted. I have labeled him the problem child. Sarah was frustrated, because she was phyically past her childbearing years, yet Abram had been given the promise of direct descendants that would outnumber the stars. She thought that, if Abraham was to have a son, they must have one the culturally acceptable way. In the day of Abraham and Sarah, it was the custom for barren women to persuade a handmaid to carry and birth a baby for them. Then the barren woman and the father of the child would adopt and raise the child as their own. This was the way in which Ishmael was conceived. Sarah encouraged her husband to have Ishmael by Hagar, an Egyptian handmaid. But after the birth of Isaac (God's promised child to Sarah), Ishmael was a constant reminder to Sarah that she had sinned by acting on her own. Therefore, she had to get him out of her sight.

Genesis 17:1-21 says:

> *And when Abram was ninety years old and nine, the Lord appeared to Abram, and said unto him, I am the Almighty God; walk before me, and be thou perfect. And I will make my covenant between me and thee, and will multiply thee exceedingly. And*

Abram fell on his face: and God talked with him, saying, As for me, behold, my covenant is with thee, and thou shalt be a father of many nations. Neither shall thy name any more be called Abram, but thy name shall be Abraham; for a father of many nations have I made thee. And I will establish my covenant between me and thee and thy seed after thee in their generations for an everlasting covenant, to be a God unto thee, and to thy seed after thee. And I will give unto thee, and to thy seed after thee, the land wherein thou art a stranger, all the land of Canaan, for an everlasting possession; and I will be their God. And God said unto Abraham, Thou shalt keep my covenant therefore, thou, and thy seed after thee in their generations. This is my covenant, which ye shall keep, between me and you and thy seed after thee; Every man child among you shall be circumcised. And ye shall circumcise the flesh of your foreskin; and it shall be a token of the covenant betwixt me and you. And he that is eight days old shall be circumcised among you, every man child in your generations, he that is born in the house, or bought with money of any stranger which is not of thy seed. He that is born in thy house, and he that is bought with thy money, must needs be circumcised: and my covenant shall be in your flesh for an everlasting covenant. And the uncircumcised man child whose flesh of his foreskin is not circumcised, that soul shall be cut off from his people; he hath broken my covenant. And God said unto Abraham, As for Sarai, thy wife, thou shalt not call her name Sarai, but Sarah shall her name be. And I will bless her, and give thee a son also of her: yea, I will bless her, and she shall be a mother of nations;

kings of people shall be of her. Then Abraham fell upon his face, and laughed, and said in his heart, Shall a child be born unto him that is an hundred years old? and shall Sarah, that is ninety years old, bear? And Abraham said unto God, O that Ishmael might live before thee! And God said, Sarah thy wife shall bear thee a son indeed; and thou shalt call his name Isaac: and I will establish my covenant with him for an everlasting covenant, and with his seed after him. And as for Ishmael, I have heard thee: Behold, I have blessed him, and will make him fruitful, and will multiply him exceedingly; twelve princes shall he beget, and I will make him a great nation. But my covenant will I establish with Isaac, which Sarah shall bear unto thee at this set time in the next year.

There is no doubt Abraham believed Ishmael to be the promised seed, but God made it clear that the seed was on its way and that the seed would be born of Sarah.

God made a special covenant with Abraham: that his son Isaac would be the promised seed, and from that blessed seed God would fulfill His promises to Abraham. But, there would be another group of princes that would also have God's interests. However, the chosen seed would definitely be through Isaac.

But let's discuss the child, Ishmael, and his seed. Let's discover who these people become.

Genesis 17:20 *"And as for Ishmael, I have heard thee: Behold, I have blessed him, and will make him fruitful, and will multiply him exceedingly; twelve princes shall he beget, and I will make him a great nation."*

God did not forget about the other child of Abraham. Ishmael would be blessed also, but not in the same way. God did bless Ishmael with twelve sons who would become a great people, but we must read on to see what would become of these descendants. God would bless them but they would be a people that would be difficult to contend with. All other nations would struggle with them.

Genesis 21:8-21 says:

> *And the child grew, and was weaned: and Abraham made a great feast the same day that Isaac was weaned. And Sarah saw the son of Hagar the Egyptian, which she had born unto Abraham, mocking. Wherefore she said unto Abraham, Cast out this bondwoman and her son: for the son of this bondwoman shall not be heir with my son, even with Isaac. And the thing was very grievous in Abraham's sight because of his son. And God said unto Abraham, let it not be grievous in thy sight because of the lad, and because of thy bondwoman; in all that Sarah hath said unto thee, hearken unto her voice; for in Isaac shall thy seed be called. And also of the son of the bondwoman will I make a nation, because he is thy seed. And Abraham rose up early in the morning, and took bread, and a bottle of water, and gave it unto Hagar, putting it on her shoulder, and the child, and sent her away: and she departed, and wandered in the wilderness of Beersheba. And the water was spent in the bottle, and she cast the child under one of the shrubs. And she went and sat her down over against him a good way off, as it were a bowshot: for she said, Let me not see the death of the child, And she sat over against him, and lifted*

> *up her voice, and wept. And God heard the voice of the lad; and the angel of God called to Hagar out of heaven, and said unto her, What aileth thee, Hagar? Fear not; for God hath heard the voice of the lad where he is. Arise, lift up the lad, and hold him in thine hand; for I will make him a great nation. And God opened her eyes, and she saw a well of water; and she went, and filled the bottle with water, and gave the lad drink. And God was with the lad; and he grew, and dwelt in the wilderness, and became an archer. And he dwelt in the wilderness of Paran: and his mother took him a wife out of the land of Egypt.*

Yes, God did provide for the other son of Abraham.

Genesis 25:12-18 gives us a little more of God's completion of His promise to Hagar about her son.

> *Now these are the generations of Ishmael, Abraham's son, whom Hagar the Egyptian, Sarah's handmaid, bare unto Abraham: And these are the names of the sons of Ishmael, by their names, according to their generations: the firstborn of Ishmael, Nebajoth; and Kedar, and Adbeel, and Mibsam, And Mishma, and Dumah, and Massa, Hadar, and Tema, Jetur, Naphish, and Kedemah: These are the sons of Ishmael, and these are their names, by their towns, and by their castles; twelve princes according to their nations. And these are the years of the life of Ishmael, an hundred and thirty and seven years: and he gave up the ghost and died; and was gathered unto his people. And they dwelt from Havilah unto Shur, that is before Egypt, as thou goest toward Assyria and he died in the presence of all his brethren.*

These princes (who represent the children of Ishmael) became nations of their own. It is understood that these twelve princes make up the Arabian nations east of Jerusalem. There is an interesting study to be made in tracking these sons of Ishmael. This would be an interesting study that will have to be done on another day, and in another book. However, it is important to note that these princes' sons and grandsons appear sporadically throughout the Bible and in the history books. It is clear that both sons of Abraham are used by God to bring about His will. They both play an important role in the unfolding of God's plan. Therefore, my focus is Isaac's seed, but occasionally the Ishmaelites will appear.

God's word does not point out a great deal about Ishmael's seed, but they always seem to dwell in the area of Arabia. They have lived primarily as nomads with only a few exceptions. They still are mainly concentrated in the area east of Jerusalem.

The last time Ishmael makes an appearance on the pages of scripture is in Genesis 25:7-11 as Isaac and Ishmael came together to bury Abraham. They parted peacefully and then Ishmael seemed to just blend into the scenery. But Isaac's children became the central focus of the scriptures.

It is important to note God's concern in relation to the descendants of Abraham called Ishmaelites.

Genesis 16:11-12, *"And the angel of the LORD said unto her, Behold, thou art with child, and shalt bear a son, and shalt call his name Ishmael; because the LORD hath heard thy affliction, And he will be a wild man; his hand will be against every man, and every man's hand against him; and he shall dwell in the presence of all his brethren."*

God raised up a group of people that would find themselves at odds with most of the world. In light of the events of today with the Middle-Eastern troubles, as well as the terror alerts all over the world, Ishmael's children have truly lived up to God's proclamation. The children of Ishmael are the Middle-Eastern nations of Iran, Iraq, Saudi Arabia, etc., I realize the Middle-Eastern countries have people other than Ishmaelites or Israelites mixed into the population there, but it is the relationship between these two people groups that is the concern of this book. (The sons of Ishmael and Isaac are at the center of the controversy.) Ishmael and Isaac are a very large part of the ongoing struggles of the world today. It seems God allowed this struggle and conflict to cause people to focus on this part of the world and cause them to wonder why they just cannot get along.

Remember the key questions:

- **Is there a God?**
- **If so, does He have a reason for creating the people called the Jews?**
- **Is He manipulating the events of the world to serve His purposes?**
- **To what extent has He already determined what has taken place and will take place in this world?**

We must return to Ishmael's seed to find the answers.

As we discuss the Ishmaelites and their hostility toward Israel, it must be noted that they now have become at odds with most other races and nations as well. This dispute with Israel and now others has caused God's Word to be examined by many looking for answers to why these groups of people are at odds with much of the rest of the world.

God said they would be at odds with all (Genesis 16). But what happened that caused their alienation? The vehicle is very easy to recognize in our day of world reporting. It is their religion – the religion of Islam. I'm sure that no one could have predicted the impact of the religion of Islam at its beginning. Let's discuss the religion of Islam just briefly.

In our day of struggles over Middle-Eastern religions and wars fought over beliefs, it is imperative that we know about this religion called Islam and those people who preach the Muslim faith.

One might think in our day of tolerance that we are not to say anything that will offend other religions or people of other races. But we must tell the facts. We must discuss the very truths that are so evident to a student of history or the Bible. This information is so clear. We really must be blind or deluded not to notice the problems that exist. The question in everyone's mind is, "Why?"

Let us explore why this happened. We must go back and see what happened to develop this religion called Islam and see its origin.

The religion of Islam began as a result of one of Ishmael's offspring, and still is primarily governed and promoted by Ishmaelites. Some of the leaders of major terrorist groups that are terrorizing the world today are Ishmaelites.

How did this religion begin?

History tells us that the founder of the religion of Islam was a man named Muhammad. He lived from 570-632

A.D. He was born into the Kareish tribe at Mecca in Arabia. At first, he was called Ubu'l Kassim, later entitled Muhammad, meaning "the Praised One." His father died two months before his birth, and his mother died when he was six years old. He was reared first by a grandfather and then by an uncle. He eventually became a nomad like his ancestors, and joined a caravan. At the age of twenty-five, he became the chief merchant and camel driver for a rich widow, Khadija, whom he married three years later. In his business enterprises, he visited Palestine and Syria, where he met Arabians, Jews and Christians. He conversed often with them about God. It is said that he had a reputation for honesty and justice that was well-founded. Finally, with four others, he vowed to take the part of the oppressed.

He decided that there had to be more to the world of religion than what he had heard. This prompted him to seek a deeper understanding of God. He decided that there was only one god, that his name was Allah, and that salvation required submission to him. With this conviction, he committed himself to the service of the "one true god" and received an urgent call to be his prophet. He recognized other prophets such as Adam, Abraham, Moses and Jesus, but believed himself to be the final prophet to whom the <u>complete</u> revelation was given. He described a vision where a voice spoke to him saying, "Iqra" (recite), certain verses. This would become the beginning of the Qur'an we know of today. His wife, Khadija, nephew, Ali, and another man named Zaid (who had been adopted by him) promptly accepted his revelations, which came over a period of three years.

In the first year of his mission, he won only eight converts, who assembled in his home and prayed faithfully to Allah.

After three years, with scarcely twenty followers, he publicly declared his purpose to overthrow the 360 idols, replacing them with the worship of his god, Allah (the one true god in his eyes). Muhammad then persecuted, boycotted and segregated the citizens of Yathrib (later called al-Medina, "the city of the prophet"), they then received him as their ruler. He eventually took flight from Mecca to a mountain cave. This trip is known as the hijra or hejira, and initiated the era and calendar of Islam, July 16, 622 A.D.

At Medina, by eloquent preaching, he converted the whole city except the Jews. He became a dictator upon a six fold pledge: (1) we will not worship any other god but the one true god; (2) we will not steal; (3) we will not commit adultery; (4) we will not kill our children; (5) we will not slander in anywise; (6) nor will we disobey the prophets in anything that is right. He built a mosque for daily prayers for the congregation to worship. He carried out a thorough program of military and religious education, attached caravans from Mecca, and defeated Mecca armies in decisive battles.

When Mecca surrendered, he became its dictator at the age of sixty. His first act was to abolish the idols; a reform which has survived in Islam to this day. Through his military victory, he changed from a prophet to a conquering ruler. He persecuted the Jews who refused to accept his religion, and reduced Christians to dependence by measures of intimidation. He sent messengers to the four great empires of Abyssinia, Egypt, Greece and Persia. Those messengers demanded allegiance to the faith, and when they refused, he conquered them by unifying the Arabian nations against them and invading. Two years later, he died (632 A.D.), but his armies marched on in fanatical zeal until they conquered three continents.

As a prophet, Muhammad envisioned one god and one brotherhood of the faith. He had the conviction and the courage to attack evil (as he saw it) and proclaim his message. As a statesman, he was vigorous, astute, determined and irresistible. He won and organized his followers by a contagious purpose, and concentrated it into a compact moral force. He was faithful to his family and friends until his first wife died. Then he provided himself with a harem and attacked his enemies with fury and deception. The force of his personality continues to influence the millions of his devoted followers.

Muhammad announced himself as the prophet of the one true god, Allah. Numerous references to Hebrew and Christian traditions indicate unquestionably his indebtedness to these faiths. For a time, he allied himself with the Jews and Christians, declaring the same God, honoring many of the same prophets, and facing Jerusalem in prayer. The primitive religions of Arabia and Zoroastrianism were other sources providing content for the new faith taking form in the dynamic mind of Muhammad. Yet the prophet did not borrow slavishly from any source; and whatever passed through the crucible of his experience came forth transformed. Islam is less dependent upon Judaism than is Christianity. Before long Muhammad turned from Jerusalem to Mecca, and the breach among these religions widened to a chasm.

The Muslim faith (iman) rests first in the basic conviction of one god and no other. Allah is addressed in prayer by ninety-nine names. His attributes include being all-seeing, all-hearing, all-speaking, all-knowing, all-willing, and all-powerful. He is loving, compassionate and forgiving, yet stern in punishment and arbitrary in purpose. In Islam, angels are associated with god; they support his throne, guard Hell, and serve as intermediaries. The four chief angels are Gabriel, who brings revelations; Michael, guardian of the Jews; Raphael (Azrael), the angel of death; and Uriel (Israfil), who is to sound the trumpet at the resurrection. There are also good and evil spirits (jinn or genii).

The chief source of revelation is sacred scriptures and prophets. Of 1,044 sacred books, four are thought to have survived. These four are the Pentateuch, the Psalms, the Gospel and the Qur'an. The Qur'an is so final that no other book is needed. It is the created word of god, eternally preserved on tablets in Heaven, and revealed to Muhammad by Gabriel. Many prophets are referred to by Muhammad and they are as high in number as 300,000. The six chief prophets are Adam, Noah, Abraham, Moses, Jesus and Muhammad, each commissioned to proclaim a new dispensation. Muhammad, the last and greatest of the prophets, is predicated by all of these.

The teaching of eschatology (last things) is an elaborate portrayal of the final judgment: Heaven and Hell. The souls of unbelievers will be tortured in Hell until the resurrection at the end of the world. The belief is that when the trumpet sounds and the graves are opened, the good and evil deeds are weighed in the balance, and everyone must pass over Hell on a bridge finer than a hair and sharper than a sword. As the righteous enter Heaven, they will be invited to feasting, music, fine garments, perfume, and large-eyed maidens.

The five duties (dim) laid upon Muslims are: (1) profession of faith, repeating the creed daily; (2) prayer five times every twenty-four hours facing Mecca; (3)

almsgiving, or the payment of poor-rates; (4) fasting every day from dawn to dusk in the month of Ramadan; and (5) a pilgrimage to Mecca at least once in a lifetime.

The civil and criminal laws arise from the Qur'an and the Sunnah. Circumcision is practiced, and four wives are allowed. The husband may divorce a wife by declaration and refunding part of her dowry. Alcoholic beverages, pork, and meat offered to idols, strangled, or killed by a blow are prohibited. The unity and traditionalism of Islam are deeply affected by the upheaval of modern civilization.

Note: it seems Muhammad's own words were to take care of the oppressed. You might wonder what Muhammad would think of the terrorist bombers and those who encourage them. It seems they have missed something, as they kill many without discrimination. It is also important to note that Allah means "Compassionate One." Where is the compassion in these terrorist acts?

Another important note is that Muhammad declared that he worshipped the same God as the Jews and Christians. However, it is clear that these are not the thoughts of the modern Muslim. Even today, there are those who believe we worship the same God.

The religion of Islam is somewhat similar to Judaism and Christianity, in that many of the same people are mentioned in its beginning: Adam, Noah, Moses, Jesus, etc. They also believe in Heaven, Hell and a future trumpet blast that will bring everyone before God for a final judgment. But, we must remember the story of Cain and Abel, the two religions of the world – Cain's way of works or Abel's way of trusting on the work of the lamb. In which category must we place the Islamic faith? The

Cain way, of course, because it relies only on man's works in this world.

Let's discuss some of those differences by inserting a portion of the book, *Unveiling Islam*, a book that speaks directly about these differences.

"There are distinct differences between the teachings of Muhammad and Christ Jesus. Remember, it is the sacrifice of the Lamb that takes away sin, not man's own works. It is also important to note that the God of the Bible and the god worshipped by Muhammad have many distinct differences.

God Loves You! This is the brash claim of Christianity. The key is to win people to a saving faith in Jesus Christ as Savior, yet in the Qur'an, no such statement is to be found. There are some simple similarities in the message. Whereas the Bible teaches that God hates sin but loves sinners (e.g. Prov. 6:16-19; Jer. 4:4; Rom 1:18; James 4:4), Islamic scripture affirms that Allah hates sinners: "For Allah loves not transgressors" (Surah 2:190).

Please note the comparisons from the Bible and the Qur'an.

The Bible says:

For God so loved the world that He gave His only begotten Son, that whosoever believes in Him should not perish but have everlasting life' (John 3:16).

'These things I have written to you who believe in the name of the Son of God, that you may know that you have eternal life' (1 John 5:13).

'But God demonstrates His own love toward us, in that while we were yet sinners, Christ died for us' (Rom 5:8).

The Qur'an says:

'And spend of your substance in the cause of Allah, and make not your own hands contribute to destruction, but do good; For Allah loves those who do good' (Surah 2:195).

'Say: "If you do love Allah, follow me: Allah will love and forgive you your sins: For Allah is Oft-forgiving, Most Merciful"' (Surah 3:31).

'Say: "Obey Allah and His Messenger:" But if they turn back, Allah loves not those who reject Faith' (Surah 3:32).

The greatest difference between the two faiths is the personal quality of God.

Allah sent prophets and messengers to proclaim the truth. In Christianity, God the Father sent His Son to be the Truth, to die for sin, and to reconcile men and women to Him. In Islam, it is hoped that salvation is earned through one's good works (Surah 3:31). One must love Allah in order to be accomplished. Good works can only give one hope for heaven, but never the guarantee of such. Since God is removed from the equation, the question of whether one is admitted to heaven is left unanswered until the Day of Judgment. For the Christian, judgment came on the cross, an event rejected by Muhammad and Islam.

We sent not a messenger except (to teach) in the language of his (own) people, in order to make (things) clear to them. So Allah leads astray those whom he pleases and guides whom he pleases and he is exalted in power, full of wisdom (Surah 14:4).

Allah is exalted and pleased as he sends people to hell; this is the fatalistic claim of Islam. Fatalism is a belief that events are fixed in advance for all time in such a manner that human beings are powerless to change them.

In this case, Allah will send to heaven whomever he pleases and send to hell whomever he pleases.

No wonder there is no security in Islam. One can be the most faithful of all believers in Allah and still rightly be sent to hell. Paradoxically, someone can be the worst person in the world, and, hypothetically, still go to paradise. One needs to look no further than Islam's founder, Muhammad, to see the anxiety and insecurity that such a view produces.

Muhammad said: 'By Allah, though I am the Apostle of Allah, yet I do not know what Allah will do to me,' (Hadith 5:266).

Muhammad questioned his own salvation, even though he was the greatest of prophets, the apostle of Allah himself. Therefore, how could Muslims have any real sense of security when the one who gave them their faith (or as the Muslim says, 'restored the truth to them') was himself apprehensive?

The Muslim is commanded in the Qur'an to 'Obey God and his apostle' (Surah 3:32) and to follow his 'exemplar (example).' As a result, the more devoutly one understands the Qur'an and follows the exemplar, the less certain one will be of reaching Paradise. Further, the more sensitive one is to his or her moral failures, the more spiritually anxious one must become.[2]

That is because Muhammad himself, the example, is unsure of the strength of his own faith. One cannot receive conviction from a leader who himself is uncertain.

It is important to note that the Islamic faith is very, very different from Christianity. The Christian has security in knowing God through the person of Jesus Christ. The

Christian's faith is in the Lamb, Jesus, Who was slain for us. We trust in His finished work to establish our righteousness. We only need to refer to the story of Cain and Abel. We are trusting, as Abel did, in the work of the Lamb. The Muslim is putting his faith in his own good works, good deeds and sacrifices. Is this not a clear picture of the Cain and Abel story in Genesis? I hope you see the importance of the stories of the first pages of the Bible.

But, to return to Muhammad, we must make note of his abilities. He took an idea and forced it on the world, and he was very successful at it. It almost seems that there had to be some force pushing this religion along. It seems God allowed this religion to thrive for some future use. What purpose to the eternal plan of God could be served by a religion that sets its heart against Jews and Christians? We need only tune in to today's news where we find, it seems, that Muslims are against everyone, especially Christians. It is the Holy Wars all over again. The Jews are right in the middle of the conflict. As a result of the conquest of Palestine by Muhammad, they have the Mosque of Omar in the middle of the temple mound in Jerusalem. All of these things are a part of God's plan. Soon we will see the full revelation of this plan.

Amazingly, Abraham is the father of three worldwide religious: Judaism, Christianity and Islam. However, the only fathering he did in the Islamic religion is to have fathered Ishmael, who fathered the Arab nations, which, in turn, fathered Muhammad, who founded the Islamic religion.

Israel is always on the front page of newspapers worldwide because of controversy. God seems to raise up an enemy against His underdog, the Jewish people, to bring attention back to the pages of the Bible. He has created the Jews so that the world will know that there is a God who is predicting all of the world's events, especially the events pertaining to the nation of Israel. Therefore, the world will hear of the Christ who came and said He would come again. In studying these events highlighted by Israel's troubles, attention is constantly focused on the Jews and the Jew called Jesus.

- **Is there a God?**
- **If so, does He have a reason for creating the people called the Jews?**
- **Is He manipulating the events of the world to serve His purpose?**
- **To what extent has He already determined what has taken place and will take place in this world?**

We cannot answer these questions without understanding how God has responded to the Jews through the years.

That brings us to our next question.

QUESTION # 6

What happens when God's chosen people reject God for the gods of the world?

It wasn't long after the Israelites received their Promised Land that they began to experience trouble with God. They quickly became discontent after leaving Egypt. They were unable to remain totally committed to the God who rescued them. While Moses was up on the mountain getting the Law of God in Exodus, we find the Israelites were even then trying to find a way to worship another god (other than the God who created and delivered them). Because of the weakness of their faith, they were unable or unwilling to find the Promised Land. God, therefore, permitted this generation to die (except for Joshua and Caleb) before He allowed the Israelites to go into the Promised Land. These two had proven themselves faithful to God, so they were the exceptions. The book of Judges reveals that, even after they possessed the Promised Land, they were continually serving themselves over God. The last verse in Judges notes the weakness of their hearts, *"In those days there was no king in Israel: every man did that which was right in his own eyes."* (Judges 21:25). This rejection of God manifested itself continually in the errors of the kings. The people were confused and inconsistent. At times, they would serve God only to revert to their own selfish ways later. Their beliefs appeared to rest on which prophets were in favor at the time. But it still is clear that they were having a hard time glorifying God in the land of promise. Therefore, God judged them by using the armies around them to come and defeat, kill, steal from, and even take Israelites captive. Their neighboring enemies brought them back to unity and humility before God. They were finally led back to their land in the days of Ezra and Nehemiah. It was then that they built the second temple in Jerusalem. This temple would be the very temple where Jesus would be dedicated. It is also important because Jesus visited it at age twelve. Isaiah 61 tells us of Jesus' visit at age thirty. If you remember your scriptures, it is the time Jesus overturned the money tables that had desecrated His temple. The Jews did return to the land after captivity. This was not to be permanent, because they were yet to be scattered again. They were to be scattered one more time before they would come into possession of this land for the final time on this planet. But they were and still are the chosen people of God. Their commitment to God was weak and wavering. Still, God made them a promise that He would give them a land, and He kept that promise. This is a testimony of the power of God's Word! But their rejection of God *as* God, and God's response to their rejection tells us that God will judge those who reject Him. Even His chosen people are not free from His judgment.

God subjected His people to different lands in order to teach them valuable lessons. He used the land and its inhabitants to teach the Israelites, just as He used quail to teach them in the days of Moses and the children of Israel in the wilderness. Numbers chapter 11 tells of this lesson. They were complaining of lack of meat in the wilderness, and He showered them with quail until they were sick of it. It seems as though God said, "Oh, you like quail, do you?"

His people continually wanted to be like the Gentile nations, desiring to follow their gods. On occasion, God would get tired of His people pulling in the world's direction, and He seemed to say, "Oh, you like their life, do you? Then live with them a while and we will see what you think of their life." But, of course, when they got there, they were abused and mistreated, and after a while, they were begging God to deliver them.

It is clear that the Gentile nations were used by God to teach the Jews the difference between walking in God's presence and living outside of it. However, it needs to be noted that God used the Gentile nations on occasion to shield Israel from danger. A great example of this was Joseph, Mary and Jesus in Matthew 2:13. This was the Christmas story, and the place Joseph hid away from Herod was Egypt.

As we just saw, the people of God were placed in the land of promise by His own hand. But when they chose to serve other gods, He chose to disperse them to other lands.

The nation of Israel has been scattered to other lands twice in their history. The first time was when they moved to Babylon. The second time was when they were dispersed to the rest of the world after they rejected Jesus, the very Son of God. A closer look at their rejection of Christ in the day of their kings is illuminating.

The people of Israel were warned in the prophesies of Ezekiel, Jeremiah, Isaiah, and others. All of the Old Testament prophets spent their lives trying to get the people of God to return to Him and receive blessings, rather than the wrath of God.

But the convictions of these men and their words fell on deaf ears. The prophets themselves many times suffered great hardships at the hands of the Israelite people. This occurred because they refused to listen to God's Word. Therefore, God gave them over to be dominated, abused, and even enslaved by the Babylonians and then the Assyrians and Medes. Eventually, they were set free to return to their homeland, but not until they had been humbled by their captors.

When they returned to rebuild the land of Canaan from Babylon, it was in such poor condition, they simply wept to think their land could be in such a plundered state. Their zeal soon began to wither and they did not follow through on their calling to rebuild their city. Then God simply went silent. During the four hundred years between the Old and New Testaments, God didn't send a prophet or His Word. We begin the second testament, the New Testament, in Matthew, with the people of God being suppressed by the Roman Empire. Jesus was born during Roman suppression. He lived for 33 years, ministered for three, and then died a terrible death of crucifixion at the hands of the Romans. But the Romans killed Him because the Jewish temple leaders and a loud mob rejected Him. This was the fulfillment of the Parable of the Wicked Husbandmen recorded in Matthew 21:33-46:

> *Hear another parable: There was a certain householder, which planted a vineyard, and hedged it round about, and digged a winepress in it, and built a tower, and let it out to husbandmen, and went into a far country: And when the time of the fruit drew near, he sent his servants to the husbandmen, that they might receive the fruits of it. And the husbandmen took his servants, and beat one, and killed another, and stoned another. Again, he sent other servants more than the first: and they*

did unto them likewise. But last of all, he sent unto them his son, saying, They will reverence my son. But when the husbandmen saw the son, they said among themselves, this is the heir; come, let us kill him, and let us seize on his inheritance. And they caught him, and cast him out of the vineyard, and slew him. When the lord therefore of the vineyard cometh, what will he do unto those husbandmen? They say unto him, He will miserably destroy those wicked men, and will let out his vineyard unto other husbandmen, which shall render him the fruits in their seasons. Jesus saith unto the, Did ye never read in the scriptures, the stone which the builders rejected, the same is become the head of the corner: this is the Lord's doing, and it is marvelous in our eyes? Therefore say I unto you, The kingdom of God shall be taken from you, and given to a nation bringing forth the fruits thereof. And whosoever shall fall on this stone shall be broken: but on whomsoever it shall fall, it will grind him to powder. And when the chief priests and Pharisees had heard his parables, they perceived that he spake of them. But when they sought to lay hands on him, they feared the multitude, because they took him for a prophet.

Matthew 22 also illustrates this same story, this time using the setting of a Jewish wedding. Those who refused to come to it would be cast away, and the highways and the hedges would be searched to find people to attend.

There are many other passages that demonstrate that the Jewish people would reject God's bold, loving invitation and another (the Gentiles) would be brought in their place.

The second time the nation of Israel was dispersed was after their rejection of Jesus and His ascension into Heaven. Scripture reveals that Jesus predicted the events to come in Luke 21:5-6, Matthew 24:1-2, and Mark 13:1-2. Jesus declared that the temple they were so proud of would be torn down, and there would not be one stone left upon another. This happened in 70 A.D. when Titus the Mede came in by Roman orders and killed a multitude of the Jewish people to stop an uprising. In the process his men set the temple on fire and burned it, but the stones were still standing. The gold in the dome of the temple however, melted, and his men turned over every stone to get out the gold that melted into the rocks, thus bringing to pass the prediction of Christ. The scripture that I would like to reference is in Luke 19:42-44, which says, *"Saying, If thou hadst known even thou, at least in this thy day, the things which belong unto thy peace! But now they are hid from thine eyes. For the days shall come upon thee, that thine enemies shall cast a trench about thee, and compass thee round, and keep thee in one every side. And shall lay thee even with the ground, and thy children within thee; and they shall not leave in thee one stone upon another; because thou knewest not the time of thy visitation."* These verses state that the city of Jerusalem was in for a day of judgment because they did not receive Him. This point was also made as Jesus stood over Jerusalem and wept in Luke 13:34-35 as He said, *"O Jerusalem, Jerusalem, which killest the prophets and stonest them that are sent unto thee; how often would I have gathered thy children together, as a hen doth gather her brood under her wings, and ye would not! Behold your house is left unto you desolate: and verily I say unto you, Ye shall not see me, until the time come when ye shall say, Blessed is he that cometh in the name of the Lord."* Yes, trouble is coming because you rejected me. Jesus even made a statement of prediction while in route to the cross as He was led up the hill to Calvary to a group of women in Luke 23:26-31:

And as they led him away, they laid hold upon one Simon, a Cyrenian, coming out of the country, and on him they laid the cross, that he might bear it after Jesus. And there followed him a great company of people, and of women, which also bewailed and lamented him. But Jesus turning unto them said, Daughters of Jerusalem, weep not for me, but weep for yourselves, and for your children. For, behold, the days are coming, in the which they shall say, Blessed are the barren, and the wombs that never bare, and the paps which never gave suck. Then shall they begin to say to the mountains, Fall on us; and to the hills, Cover us. For if they do these things in a green tree, what shall be done in the dry?

Jesus was saying that the days ahead were going to be troubled days for the people of the city of Jerusalem. He told of troubled times ahead, and there is no question that the Jews have reaped consequences as a result of their disobedience. It was so bad that those who were not killed were scattered all over the world to live for a long period of time, almost two thousand years, before they came home.

The point is, when God's people reject Him, they pay a great price for that rejection. Their lack of faith caused them to walk around in the heat of the desert for forty years in the days of Moses' leadership. Their rejection of God and their desire to serve the gods of the Gentiles in the days of the kings brought seventy years of servanthood in the city of Babylon and surrounding areas. Then when the Jewish leaders and those who listened to them rejected God's Son, they were delivered into the hands of an abusive Gentile world of cruelty for a time. While it is true they would be preserved as a people, they would be treated miserably and scattered all over the world. This leads us to the next question.

QUESTION # 7

Will God be angry at Israel forever?

*He will not always chide:
neither will he keep his anger forever.*

Psalm 103:9

The answer is no! Let me explain through a historical perspective.

After the forty years of wilderness, Joshua brought the people of God into their Promised Land. They finally took possession of the land that Abraham had walked for many years. Finally, in God's time, they came to possess it. However, as previously discussed, they would not keep it. They would be dragged off into the land of the Babylonians and they would spend seventy hard and painful years there. Only then would they be humbled before God and returned to their own land.

The return of the Israelites to their land was a trying challenge for them. First, their neighbors did not want them. Second, the Israelites had difficulty just staying on task. God intervened and, through a few determined leaders, they did possess and rebuild the city of Jerusalem and the walls again. This was the second time they were in possession of their land.

Zerubbabel, Ezra and Nehemiah were burdened to take groups to the ruins and rebuild it. It took many years and much toil but they did accomplish their goal. They were back in their land and functioning as a country again, but it wasn't like it once was. They accomplished this feat by a miraculous acceptance of God in the heart of Artaxerxes, the king of the Persian Empire around 445 B.C.

They stayed in the land, but continued to struggle with the problem of staying in harmony with God. Malachi was the last Old Testament prophet, and he was very disturbed about the heartless effort toward worship by God's chosen people. When the Romans came along, we find that the Jewish people were in their land, but ordered around by the Romans. They found they could only worship with Roman permission. Then Jesus was born in a manger in Bethlehem. He grew up under Roman oppression, and even died at the hands of the Roman soldiers. After the death, burial, resurrection and ascension of Jesus, only a few years later, the Jews were again scattered -- to the four winds of the Earth. Yes, the Jewish people once again were expelled from the Promised Land. This time they would be out of their homeland almost two thousand years. They would be abused in almost every way possible, killed in record numbers (and not just in one area). Only after these ordeals and persistent persecution would they be allowed to return. Many prophecies told of the abuses that were ahead of them, and many prophecies told of their eventual return. Both came true in a bold declaration.

Even before the first departure of Israel out of the Promised Land, God knew that they would be back. He knew how long they would be gone, and that it would not be the last time they would have to leave their homeland. But in the end, they will finish out the Earth's time of existence back in their land, with the Son of God ruling the world from the throne of Jerusalem.

There were major events planned in God's own time that would lead up to the eventual rule of God's Son from Jerusalem's throne. Some of those major events were:

- The birth of Isaac
- The birth of Moses and the Jewish deliverance under his leadership
- The eventual possession of the Promised Land achieved by Joshua
- The Davidic kingdom and Jerusalem becoming the capital city of Israel
- The first temple built by Solomon
- The carrying away to Babylon and the destruction of the temple
- The return to rebuild the city commissioned by Artaxerxes
- The birth of Jesus under the Romans, and His life, death, resurrection and ascension
- The coming of the Holy Spirit to the New Testament Church in Acts 2
- The Church age
- The coming of a move to regather in Jerusalem
- The Jews will be a burdensome stone

The regathering actually began after World War II, when on November 29, 1947, the United Nations General Assembly passed a resolution calling for the establishment of a Jewish state. A copy of this document for those who may be interested may be found in the Encyclopedic Dictionary of Judaica, published by Keter Publishing House, Jerusalem Israel, in 1974.

This declaration opened the door for a new Jewish state.

These are exciting events! Never in the history of the world have events such as this ever been recorded to have happened. God has continually shown His involvement in the lives of the Jewish people. Again, we must recognize God and His involvement in the events that have transpired in the lives of the Jews.

Let us now return to answer the question posed at the beginning of this section. Will God be angry at Israel forever?

God has great plans for Israel. He scattered and tried them in order to humble them before Him. But He has always held a special place for them. Now God is regathering His chosen people. They will be home now when He comes to rule the world from their city.

QUESTION # 8

What happened to the people of God when they rejected God's only begotten Son?

The Jews' rejection of Christ has already been addressed. However, understanding the event of that rejection is important.

There are many prophecies that reference the Son of God being rejected by the people of God. History shows us the heavy price the Jews have paid for disobedience. Let's review just a few of the references to His rejection. Note the price paid in Isaiah 61 for their rejection.

Isaiah 61:1-11 reveals to us:

> *The Spirit of the Lord God is upon me; because the LORD hath anointed me to preach good tidings unto the meek; he hath sent me to bind up the broken hearted, to proclaim liberty to the captives, and the opening of the prison to them that are bound; To proclaim the acceptable year of the LORD, and the day of vengeance of our God; to comfort all that mourn; To appoint unto them that mourn in Zion, to give unto them beauty for ashes, the oil of joy for mourning, the garment of praise for the spirit of heaviness; that they might be called trees of righteousness, the planting of the LORD,*

that he might be glorified. And they shall build the old wastes, they shall raise up the former desolations, and they shall repair the waste cities, the desolations of many generations. And strangers shall stand and feed your flocks, and the sons of the alien shall be your plowmen and your vinedressers. But ye shall be named the Priests of the LORD; men shall call you the Ministers of our God: ye shall eat the riches of the Gentiles, and in their glory shall ye boast yourselves. For your shame ye shall have double; and for confusion they shall rejoice in their portion: therefore in their land they shall possess the double: everlasting joy shall be unto them. For I the LORD love judgment, I hate robbery for burnt offering: and I will direct their work in truth, and I will make an everlasting covenant with them. And their seed shall be known among the Gentiles, and their offspring among the people: all that see them shall acknowledge them, that they are the seed which the Lord hath blessed. I will greatly rejoice in the LORD, my soul shall be joyful in my God; for he hath clothed me with the garments of salvation, he hath covered me with the robe of righteousness, as a bridegroom decketh himself with ornaments, and as a bride adorneth herself with her jewels. For as the earth bringeth forth her bud, and as the garden causeth the things that are sown in it to spring forth; so the Lord God will cause righteousness and praise to spring forth before all the nations.

The Jews are to be subjected to twice as much trouble as the Gentiles. The resulting confusion will bless the Gentiles twofold.

Early on in His ministry, Christ read these same lines in the temple at Jerusalem. He taught that the scripture had been fulfilled in front of their very eyes. He told them that the remainder of this passage was foretelling of things to come.

Sadly, we find even further evidence of the rejection of Christ.

Isaiah 53:1-12 says:

> *Who hath believed our report? And to whom is the arm of the LORD revealed? For he shall grow up before him as a tender plant, and as a root out of a dry ground: he hath no form nor comeliness; and when we shall see him, there is no beauty that we should desire him. He is despised and rejected of men: a man of sorrows, and acquainted with grief: and we hid as it were our faces from him; he was despised, and we esteemed him not. Surely he hath borne our griefs, and carried out sorrows: yet we did esteem him stricken, smitten of God, and afflicted. But he was wounded for our transgressions, he was bruised for our iniquities: the chastisement of our peace was upon him; and with his stripes we are healed. All we like sheep have gone astray; we have turned every one to his own way; and the LORD hath laid on him the iniquity of us all. He was oppressed, and he was afflicted, yet he opened not his mouth: he is*

brought as a lamb to the slaughter, and as a sheep before her shearers is dumb, so he opened not his mouth. He was taken from prison and from judgment: and who shall declare his generation? For he was cut off out of the land of the living: for the transgression of my people was he stricken. And he made his grave with the wicked, and with the rich in his death; because he had done no violence, neither was any deceit in his mouth. Yet it pleased the LORD to bruise him: he hath put him to grief: when thou shalt make his soul an offering for sin, he shall see his seed, he shall prolong his days, and the pleasure of the LORD shall prosper in his hand. He shall see of the travail of his soul, and shall be satisfied: by his knowledge shall my righteous servant justify many; for he shall bear their iniquities. Therefore will I divide him a portion with the great, and he shall divide the spoil with the strong; because he hath poured out his soul unto death: and he was numbered with the transgressors; and he bare the sin of many, and made intercession for the transgressors.

Jesus, as well as other New Testament figures, compared these prophecies to the events of the day heralding their truth.

Matthew 8:16-17 tell us, *"When the even was come, they brought unto him many that were possessed with devils: and he cast out the spirits with his word, and healed all that were sick: That it might be fulfilled which was spoken* by Esaias [Isaiah] the prophet, saying, Himself took our infirmities, and bare our sickness."

Luke 22:37 reveals, *"For I say unto you, that this that is written must yet be accomplished in me, And he was reckoned among the transgressors: for the things concerning me have an end."*

John 12:37-41 confirms this fact, stating, *"But though he had done so many miracles before them, yet they believed not on him: That the saying of Esaias [Isaiah] the prophet might be fulfilled, which he spake, Lord, who hath believed our report? And to whom hath the arm of the Lord been revealed? Therefore they could not believe, because that Esaias [Isaiah] said again, He hath blinded their eyes, and hardened their heart; that they should not see with their eyes, nor understand with their heart, and be converted, and I should heal them. These things said Esaias [Isaiah], when he saw his glory, and spake of him."*

Hebrews 9:27-28 brings us this message stating, *"And as it is appointed unto men once to die, but after this the judgment: So Christ was once offered to bear the sins of many; and unto them that look for him shall he appear the second time without sin unto salvation."*

There are three references alone in Revelation. They are as follows:

Revelation 5:6 *"And I beheld, and lo, in the midst of the throne and of the four beasts, and in the midst of the elders, stood a lamb as it had been slain, having seven horns and seven eyes, which are the seven spirits of God sent forth into all the earth."*

Revelation 5:12-13 *"Saying with a loud voice, Worthy is the Lamb that was slain to receive power, and riches, and wisdom, and strength, and honor, and glory, and blessing. And every creature which is in heaven, and on the earth, and under the earth, and such as are in the sea, and all that are in them, heard I saying, Blessing, and honour, and glory, and power, be unto him that sitteth upon the throne, and unto the Lamb forever and ever."*

Revelation 13:8 *"And all that dwell upon the earth shall worship him, whose names are not written in the book of life of the Lamb slain from the foundation of the world."*

This is the confirmation that the lamb of the Old Testament is our Lord and Savior, Jesus Christ. Who else could possibly fulfill these prophecies? Jesus – born of the virgin Mary, born in Bethlehem, born to die. He fulfilled God's will by dying for the sins of the world.

Remember the proclamation made by the names of those ten righteous men from Adam to Noah. God allowed those ten individuals to bring comfort and peace to suffering world.

Man is appointed to a mortal end. The mighty God is to come down a mortal man and, at His death, judgment will come and sorrow. But He will comfort us.

Remember the questions:

- **Is there a God?**
- **If so, does He have a reason for creating the people called the Jews?**
- **Is He manipulating the events of the world to serve His purpose?**

- **To what extent has He already determined what has taken place and will take place in this world?**

Point to be made: The rejection of God's Son was not a surprise to God!

Yes, Israel continued to reject the goodness God sent their way.

They were exiled to Babylon and spent seventy years there under evil and ruthless leaders. This occurred after the Jews rejected God in the time of the book of the kings. Therefore, they were abused and mistreated in ways we cannot even imagine. But, there are a few things we do know. They were separated from their families, forced to become servants, thrown to lions and incinerated in ovens. Their suffering was brought on by their own rejection of God. Their idolatry displeased God and, for that, they were made to suffer.

There were Jews who did not reject Jesus the Christ. However, most of the nation did bring judgment to all. During the time of the great prophets, there were many Jews still committed to the Lord. There is a parallel to this in America today. While the voices of many Christians remain strong, the nation as a whole has turned a deaf ear to the Word of God. America must turn back to trusting the Word of God and respecting God's authority.

But remember, when the nation of Israel as a whole rejected the Son of God, they were then rejected by God and sent into hardship and bondage. Millions of Jews were killed by the Germans, but they were not the only ones who abused and killed the Jews. The Jews were scattered just as the prophets of the Old Testament had said they would be. However, there is no purpose in anger directed at God. The abuse of the Jews was not of His making, but rather allowed by Him. He lifted His protection of the Jews just as the Jews failed to protect His Son. Instead, as we know, they chose to release a criminal. Is it a coincidence that it was a war criminal such as Hitler who targeted the Jewish race? But before we feel too angry at God for allowing them to be abused in such ways, we must remember the abuse the Son of God received at the hands of the Romans, but arranged by the Jews.

The Israeli people have suffered in every generation in some way. Everyone suffers some on this planet, but no other people group has suffered at the hands of so many different groups, during every period in history. It just appears that the world has targeted the Israelites as a people to be punished.

It is thought that the Germans brought the greatest amount of suffering upon them, but many countries were involved in the abuse and slaughter of the children of Abraham. Simon Wiesenthal Center Library and Archives, in Los Angeles, California (now known as the Museum of Tolerance), gives a close estimate of the Jewish population murdered before World War II in the European Countries. It also gives the percentage of Jewish population killed in that country:

Austria	50,000	27.0%
Italy	7,680	17.3%
Belgium	28,900	44.0%
Latvia	71,500	78.1%
Bohemia/Moravia	78,150	66.1%

Lithuania	143,000	85.1%
Bulgaria	0	0.0%
Luxembourg	1,950	55.7%
Denmark	60	0.7%
Netherlands	100,000	71.4%
Norway	762	44.8%
Estonia	2,000	44.4%
Finland	7	0.3%
Poland	3,000,000	90.9%
France	77,320	22.1%
Romania	287,000	47.1%
Germany	141,500	25.0%
Slovakia	71,000	79.8%
Greece	67,000	86.6%
Hungary	569,000	69.0%
Soviet Union	1,100,000	36.4%
Yugoslavia	63,300	81.2%

It is estimated that during the Holocaust itself at least 5,860,000 Jews were killed. Six million is the round figure calculated by most authorities. For further information on this subject, log on to www.museumoftolerance.com/education/teacher-resources/holocaust-resources.

It could be said that the Jews have brought much of the suffering upon themselves in many ways. God's message to the Jews was that they would suffer if they abandoned the God Who had created them and delivered them. The Jews have paid dearly for that mistake and they are still paying.

One must realize however, that the abuse of Christ was allowed by God, and the abuse of the Jews was also allowed, but both were sad and tragic events. It is only by the grace of God that good can come out of such pain. One must be sure to realize that God has promised to bless those who bless His people. Those who were the abusers of the Jewish people of God have suffered greatly because of it, and those who have labored to bless them have been extremely blessed. God does not tell us that we are able to abuse the Jews because they abused His Son. In fact, the Bible tells us just the opposite. Therefore, one must love the Jews, bless them, pray for them, and look for every opportunity to do good to them, and God will be sure to bless you.

However, God gave us the nation of Israel as a schoolmaster to teach us the consequences of rejecting Him as God. The lesson is directed toward the nation, but the individual will not be spared the consequences.

Israel has wandered as a lost people, looking for their way. They wandered in the wilderness for forty years because they did not believe God when He told them to go into the Promised Land in the days of Moses. They wandered into the hands of their enemies in the days of the judges (Judges 3 and 4, etc.). They were given to the Babylonians, Medes and Persians, Romans, and eventually to the rest of the world. These consequences flowed from a river of disbelief. Now they are still wandering as a nation. Even though they are returning daily to the homeland, only a small group is returning to God.

But my point is that all this was predicted by God. It was not God's desire that His people reject Him. He knew their hearts, realizing that rejection would come and He would use it for His divine purpose.

Isaiah 61:7 *"For your shame ye shall have double; and for confusion they [the Gentiles] shall rejoice in their portion. Therefore in their land they shall possess the double; everlasting joy shall be unto them."*

By rejecting Jesus, the Israelites were made to suffer while the Gentiles rejoiced. By their rejection of the Messiah, the door was opened for the Gentiles to accept God's gift of salvation.

Isaiah 63:10 *"But they rebelled and vexed his Holy Spirit: therefore he was turned to be their enemy and he fought against them."*

Therefore, because the Jewish people would not heed God's plan, they suffered greatly, much as Gomer did in the story of the prophet Hosea. Hosea allowed his wife to choose her own fate for a time. God also permitted the Jews to follow their own selfish ways. Just as Hosea took Gomer back, God is waiting to take back His chosen people. God has turned to the Gentiles during this period of Jewish uncertainty, but it won't last much longer.

QUESTION # 9

Why do the Gentiles now claim to be a part of God's chosen people? Is this biblically accurate?

It was no surprise when the Gentiles came to the center of the stage of God's plan. God was clear in the prophecies about the coming day of the Gentiles.

Jesus spent almost all of His time ministering to the Jewish areas of Israel. However, on a few occasions He visited Gentile areas to minister: the Gadarene demoniac (Mark 5) and the Samaritan woman at the well (John 4) to name a few. (The Samaritans were half-Jewish, but had intermarried with Gentiles, so they were considered Gentiles.) But the best example is the visit in Matthew 15:21 or Mark 7:24-30:

> *And from thence he arose, and went into the borders of Tyre and Sidon, and entered into an house, and would have no man know it, but he could not be hid. For a certain woman, whose young daughter had an unclean spirit, heard of him, and came and fell at his feet: The woman was a Greek, a Syrophenician by nation; and she besought him that he would cast forth the devil out of her daughter. But Jesus said unto her, Let the children first be filled: for it is not meet to take the*

> *children's bread, and to cast it unto the dogs. And she answered and said unto him, Yes, Lord: yet the dogs under the table eat of the children's crumbs. And he said unto her, For this saying go thy way; the devil is gone out of thy daughter. And when she was come to her house, she found the devil gone out, and her daughter laid upon the bed.*

It was very clear that God was focused on the lost sheep of the house of Israel. But, as we have seen, they were not interested in Him. Therefore, God turned His affections to the Gentiles. Many of the parables Jesus told as He conversed with the Jewish Pharisees were explaining the future shifting of God's affections from the Jewish people if they did not heed His divine invitation. Let's look at a few of these passages with this in mind.

Matthew 21:33-46 (I realize I used this parable before, but it makes such a good point, it bears repeating):

> *Hear another parable: There was a certain householder, which planted a vineyard, and hedged it round about, and digged a winepress in it, and built a tower, and let it out to husbandmen, and went into a far country: And when the time of the fruit drew near, he sent his servants to the husbandmen, that they might receive the fruits of it. And the husbandmen took his servants, and beat one, and killed another, and stoned another. Again, he sent other servants more than the first: and they did unto them likewise. But last of all, he sent unto them his son, saying, They will reverence my son. But when the husbandmen saw the son, they said among themselves, this is the heir; come, let us kill*

> him, and let us seize on his inheritance. And they caught him, and cast him out of the vineyard, and slew him. When the lord therefore of the vineyard cometh, what will he do unto those husbandmen? They say unto him, He will miserably destroy those wicked men, and will let out his vineyard unto other husbandmen, which shall render him the fruits in their seasons. Jesus saith unto the, Did ye never read in the scriptures, the stone which the builders rejected, the same is become the head of the corner: this is the Lord's doing, and it is marvelous in our eyes? Therefore say I unto you, The kingdom of God shall be taken from you, and given to a nation bringing forth the fruits thereof. And whosoever shall fall on this stone shall be broken: but on whomsoever it shall fall, it will grind him to powder. And when the chief priests and Pharisees had heard his parables, they perceived that he spake of them. But when they sought to lay hands on him, they feared the multitude, because they took him for a prophet.

They (the Jewish leaders) realized that He was talking about them.

Luke recorded that on Palm Sunday, while Jesus was being hailed King by the crowd, the Pharisees told Him to rebuke His disciples. Instead, He made a sad statement:

Luke 19:39-44:

> And some of the Pharisees from among the multitude said unto him, Master, rebuke thy disciples. And he answered and said unto them, I

> *tell you that, if these should hold their peace, the stones would immediately cry out. And when he was come near, he beheld the city, and wept over it, Saying, If thou hadst known, even thou, at least in this thy day, the things which belong unto thy peace! But now they are hid from thine eyes. For the days shall come upon thee, that thine enemies shall cast a trench about thee, and compass thee round, and keep thee in on every side. And shall lay thee even with the ground, and thy children within thee; and they shall not leave in thee one stone upon another; because thou knewest not the time of thy visitation.*

He was predicting the future trouble for the Jewish people because of their rejection of Him.

In Matthew, chapters 23 and 24, Jesus tells of the woes that will come to the Jewish people because of their leadership's blindness, and the evil that resulted from that blindness. They have, for generations, rejected God's messengers – Matthew 23:34-36 *Wherefore, behold I send unto you prophets, and wise men, and scribes: and some of them ye shall kill and crucify, and some of them shall ye scourge in your synagogues, and persecute them from city to city: That upon you may come all the righteous blood shed upon the earth, from the blood of righteous Abel unto the blood of Zacharias son of Barachias, whom ye slew between the temple and the altar. Verily I say unto you, all these things shall come upon this generation."*

Jesus was telling the Jewish people that there was coming a day when they would weep because they once again rejected God's offer. Therefore, the woes would come.

Luke 24:26-31:

> *Ought not Christ to have suffered these things, and to enter into his glory? And beginning at Moses and all the prophets, he expounded unto them in all the scriptures the things concerning himself. And they drew night unto the village, whither they went: and he made as though he would have gone further. But they constrained him saying, Abide with us: for it is toward evening, and the day is far spent. And he went in to tarry with them. And it came to pass, as he sat at meat with them, he took bread and blessed it, and brake and gave to them. And their eyes were opened and they knew him; and he vanished out of their sight.*

As Jesus was being led to die, He was making references (even at that moment) to the coming woes that the Jewish people would inherit. His coming and dying would be a note of transfer as it pertained to the people of Israel. After His death and resurrection, the people of Israel would experience an extreme period of misery and suffering. Just as Jesus had predicted in Mark 13:1-2, Matthew 24:1-2, as well as Luke 21:5-19, the temple was destroyed and the multitudes in the land of Israel were slaughtered and died at the hands of the Roman, Titus the Mede, in 70 A.D.

Mark 13:1-2 *"And as he went out of the temple, one of his disciples saith unto him, Master, see what manner of stones and what buildings are here! And Jesus answering said unto him, Seest thou these great buildings? There shall not be left one stone upon another, that shall not be thrown down."*

Matthew 24:1-2 *"And Jesus went out, and departed from the temple: and his disciples came to him for to shew him the buildings of the temple. And Jesus said unto them, See ye not all these things? Verily I say unto you, there shall not be left here one stone upon another, that shall not be thrown down."*

Luke 21:5-19:

> *And as some spake of the temple, how it was adorned with goodly stones and gifts, he said, As for these things which ye behold, the days will come, in the which there shall not be left one stone upon another, that shall not be thrown down. And they asked him saying, Master, but when shall these things be? and what sign will there be when thee things shall come to pass? And he said, Take heed that ye be not deceived: for many shall come in my name, saying, I am Christ and the time draweth near: go ye not therefore after them. But when ye shall hear of wars and commotions, be not terrified; for these things must first come to pass; but the end is not by and by. Then said he unto them, Nation shall rise against nation, and kingdom against kingdom: And great earthquakes shall be in divers places, and famines and pestilences: and fearful sights and great signs shall there be from heaven. But before all these, they shall lay their hands on you, and persecute you, delivering you up to the synagogues, and into prisons being brought before kings and rulers for my name's sake. And it shall turn to you for a testimony. Settle it therefore in your hearts, not to*

meditate before what ye shall answer: For I will give you a mouth and wisdom, which all your adversaries shall not be able to gainsay nor resist. And ye shall be betrayed both by parents, and brethren, and kinsfolks, and friends; and some of you shall they cause to be put to death. And ye shall be hated of all men for my name's sake. But there shall not an hair of your head perish. In your patience possess ye your souls.

In three different places, the gospels tell us of the coming days of trouble for the Jews (as well as the world), but first Jesus said He would suffer and die at the hands of angry men. It is important to note that the next thing on the agenda after the death and resurrection of Christ was the persecution of the followers of Christ. We are told to look for worldly signs that will proclaim the nearing of the end of the world.

It is important to realize that Jesus will be rejected by men, the Jews will be rejected by men, and the followers of Christ will be rejected by men.

It is important to note that, after the rejection of Jesus, the focus of God will turn to the world and its people. After Jesus was rejected, the people of Israel were assaulted and scattered all over the globe, just as the prophets had predicted. They will be regathered together just before the end.

It is true; Jesus predicted the Jewish demise and the resulting new focus on God the Father. Therefore, in Acts 2, when the Spirit came to the few faithful Galileans and gave them the ability to speak the languages of people other than the Jews, it was understandable. From the time God called Abraham to be the father of His nation, as far as we know, God never spoke to a person other than a Jew until the Day of Pentecost in Acts 2. But then God used the Jewish Galileans to talk to the other races of the world. This was a milestone event because it showed the new focus of God to reach out to people other than Jewish people. Before this moment in Acts 2, God only spoke in the language of the Hebrews. Now He speaks in the languages of all people.

Acts 2:1-12:

> *And when the day of Pentecost was fully come, they were all with one accord in one place. And suddenly there came a sound from heaven as of a rushing mighty wind, and it filled all the house where they were sitting. And there appeared unto them cloven tongues like as of fire, and it sat upon each of them. And they were all filled with the Holy Ghost, and began to speak with other tongues, as the Spirit gave them utterance. And there were dwelling at Jerusalem Jews, devout men, out of every nation under heaven. Now when this was noised abroad, the multitude came together, and were confounded, because that every man heard them speak in his own language. And they were all amazed and marvelled, saying one to another, Behold, are not all these which speak Galileans? And how hear we every man in our own tongue, wherein we were born? Parthians, and Medes, and Elamites, and the dwellers in Mesopotamia, and in Judaea, and Cappadocia, in Pontus, and Asia,*

> *Phrygia, and Pamphylia, in Egypt, and in the parts of Libya about Cyrene, and strangers of Rome, Jews and proselytes, Cretes and Arabians, we do hear them speak in our tongues the wonderful works of God. And they were all amazed, and were in doubt, saying one to another, What meaneth this?*

These passages have been misunderstood for many years. But, as we see them through the eyes of the prophecies of the end, it is apparent that God's communication changed on the Day of Pentecost to reach out to all nations.

This should not be a surprise, since Jesus had given His followers the Great Commission to go to all the world and declare His message of forgiveness and eternal life, as well as His message that predicted the coming of the end.

Matthew 28:18-20 *"And Jesus came and spake unto them, saying, All power is given unto me in heaven and in earth. Go ye therefore, and teach all nations, baptizing them in the name of the Father, and of the Son, and of the Holy Ghost. Teaching them to observe all things whatsoever I have commanded you: and, lo, I am with you alway, even unto the end of the world. Amen."*

Acts 1:8 *"But ye shall receive power, after that the Holy Ghost is come upon you: and ye shall be witnesses unto me both in Jerusalem, and in all Judea, and in Samaria, and unto the uttermost part of the earth."*

These were the last words Jesus spoke before He departed. This is our task, just as it was for His disciples. Soon after He spoke these words to them, they received the Holy

Spirit and the ability to speak to the nations of the world (Acts 2).

Then, in Acts chapter 9, God called Saul of Tarsus to preach the message of Jesus to the Gentiles. Who were Gentiles? Gentiles were people who were not Jewish. There were only two types of people in the world: Jews and Gentiles. Now God was turning His affections from Israel to the Gentiles. This man, Saul, who up to this point in his life had persecuted the Christians, was himself a Jew who was raised to think these Christians were enemies of God. He then came to realize that they were the fulfillment of God's plan.

Saul eventually became known as Paul. The purpose of Paul's calling soon became common knowledge to the New Testament Church. God declared His purpose for Paul by way of the man God told him to go see; a man named Ananias, a faithful follower of God. Acts 9:15 *"But the Lord said unto him, Go thy way: for he is a chosen vessel unto me, to bear my name before the Gentiles, and kings, and the children of Israel."*

Note that Paul was to bear His name before the Gentiles, and kings, and the children of Israel. Paul became a great servant of God, declaring the Gospel of Jesus Christ to the Jews and Gentiles. In accomplishing this, God used him to write many of the New Testament Scriptures.

In Acts 10, the Apostle Peter had an amazing experience that compelled him to be willing to go and share the message of Jesus with a Gentile Roman soldier. This gave Peter a completely new understanding of God's focus. Peter then did a great deal of work in the areas where the

Gentiles lived and worked. Acts 11:1-18 records the report given by Peter (to the Church at Jerusalem) of the events in the Roman soldier's house. Therefore, the New Testament followers were beginning to focus on those other than the Jewish people. As we observe the work of God in the book of Acts in the New Testament, it is clear that God is shifting His work into a world of outreach focusing on the Gentile areas. God did not reject the Jews, but it is clear that they rejected Him. Therefore, the new focus is now on the rest of the world. From Acts 13 through the remaining chapters of Acts, Paul and others conducted three missionary journeys and wrote at least thirteen letters, mainly to the Gentiles of the world. This became quite clear in the record of the acts of the New Testament Church written by Luke. Acts 17:6 *"... These that have turned the world upside down are come hither also;"*

Other passages referencing the new focus:

In Romans 10:1-11, Paul writes that he has a desire for his people's conversion to Christ, that he would even be willing to be accursed if it would help them come to Jesus. He also tells the Jewish people that they have a zeal of God, but not according to knowledge. Paul is telling us that the Jews did not understand what was to follow the death and resurrection of Christ. They were lost as to what they must do next.

Romans 10:1-13:

> *Brethren, my heart's desire and prayer to God for Israel is, that they might be saved. For I bear them record that they have a zeal of God, but not*

according to knowledge. For they being ignorant of God's righteousness and going about to establish their own righteousness, have not submitted themselves unto the righteousness of God. For Christ is the end of the law for righteousness to everyone that believeth. For Moses describeth the righteousness which is of the law, That the man which doeth those things shall live by them. But the righteousness which is of faith speaketh on this wise, Say not in thine heart, Who shall ascend into heaven? (that is, to bring Christ down from above) Or, Who shall descend into the deep? (that is to bring up Christ again from the dead) But what saith it? The word is nigh thee, even in thy mouth, and in thy heart: that is, the word of faith, which we preach; that if thou shalt confess with thy mouth the Lord Jesus; and shalt believe in thine heart that God hath raised him from the dead, thou shalt be saved. For with the heart man believeth unto righteousness; and with the mouth confession is made unto salvation. For the scripture saith, Whosoever believeth on him shall not be ashamed. For there is no difference between the Jew and the Greek; for the same Lord over all is rich unto all that call upon him. For whosoever shall call upon the name of the Lord shall be saved.

These were bold statements about the need of Jews and Gentiles alike.

Also, in Romans 11:1-36, God declares through Paul that the casting away of the Jews blessed the world with the opportunity to be God's.

Romans 11:1-36:

> *I say, then, Hath God cast away his people? God forbid. For I also am an Israelite, of the seed of Abraham, of the tribe of Benjamin. God hath not cast away his people which he foreknew. Wot ye not what the Scripture saith of Elias? how he maketh intercession to God against Israel, saying, Lord, they have killed thy prophets, and digged down thine altars; and I am left alone, and they seek my life. But what saith the answer of God unto him? I have reserved to myself seven thousand men, who have not bowed the knee to the image of Baal. Even so then at this present time also there is a remnant according to the election of grace. And if by grace, then is it no more of works: otherwise grace is no more grace: But if it be of works, then is it no more grace: otherwise work is no more work. What then? Israel hath not obtained that which he seeketh for but the election hath obtained it, and the rest were blinded. (According as it is written, God hath given them the spirit of slumber, eyes that they should not see, and ears that they should not hear) unto this day. And David saith, Let their table be made a snare, and a trap, and a stumblingblock, and a recompense unto them: Let their eyes be darkened that they may not see and bow down their back alway. I say then, Have they stumbled that they*

should fall? God forbid: but rather through their fall salvation is come unto the Gentiles, for to provoke them to jealousy. Now if the fall of them be the riches of the world, and the diminishing of them the riches of the Gentiles; how much more their fullness? For I speak to you Gentiles, inasmuch as I am the apostle of the Gentiles, I magnify mine office: if by any means I may provoke to emulation them which are my flesh, and might save some of them. For if the casting away of them be the reconciling of the world, what shall the receiving of them be, but life from the dead? For if the firstfruit be holy, the lump is also holy: and if the root be holy, so are the branches. And if some of the branches be broken off, and thou, being a wild olive tree, wert grafted in among them, and with them partakest of the root and fatness of the olive tree; Boast not against the branches, but if thou boast, thou bearest not the root, but the root thee. Thou wilt say then, The branches were broken off, that I might be grafted in. Well; because of unbelief they were broken off, and thou standest by faith. Be not highminded, but fear: For if God spared not the natural branches, take heed lest he also spare not thee. Behold therefore the goodness and severity of God: on them which fell, severity; but toward thee, goodness, if thou continue in his goodness: otherwise thou also shalt be cut off. And they also if they abide not still in unbelief, shall be graffed in: for God is able to graft them in again. For if thou wert cut out of the olive tree which is wild by nature, and wert graffed contrary to nature into a good olive tree: how much more shall these, which be the natural branches, be graffed into their own olive tree? For I would not, brethren, that ye should be ignorant of this mystery, lest ye should be wise in your own conceits; that blindness in part is happened to Israel, until the fullness of the Gentiles be come in. And so all Israel shall be saved: as it is written, There shall come out of Sion the Deliverer, and shall turn away ungodliness from Jacob: For this is my covenant unto them, when I shall take away their sins. As concerning the gospel, they are enemies for your sakes: but as touching the election, they are beloved for the fathers' sakes. For the gifts and calling of God are without repentance. For as ye in times past have not believed God, yet have now obtained mercy through their unbelief: Even so have these also now not believed that through your mercy they also may obtain mercy. For God hath concluded them all in unbelief, that he might have mercy upon all. O the depth of the riches both of the wisdom and knowledge of God! how unsearchable are his judgments and his ways past finding out! For who hath known the mind of the Lord? or who hath been his counsellor? Or who hath first given to him, and it shall be recompensed unto him again? For of him and through him and to him, are all things: to whom be glory forever. Amen.

God is clearly saying through the Apostle Paul in verse 15 that the casting away of them (Israel) will result in the reconciliation of the world. But in verses 29-33 Paul says that God is wise and has a plan that is far wiser than we could possibly understand. Therefore, we need to trust Him for what we do not understand.

It is also clear in Acts 17:26-31, which reveals:

> *And hath made of one blood all nations of men for to dwell on all the face of the earth, and hath determined the times before appointed, and the bounds of their habitation; That they should seek the Lord, if haply they might feel after him, and find him, though he be not far from every one of us: For in him we live and move, and have our being, as certain also of your own poets have said, For we are also his offspring. Forasmuch then as we are the offspring of God, we ought not to think that the Godhead is like unto gold, or silver, or stone, graven by art and man's device. And the times of this ignorance God winked at; but now commandeth all men every where to repent: because he hath appointed a day in the which he will judge the world in righteousness by that man whom he ordained; whereof he hath given assurance unto all men, in that he hath raised him from the dead.*

Therefore, because of the death, burial and resurrection of Christ, all of mankind is responsible to turn to God through the way Christ has made. It has allowed both Jews and Gentiles to find salvation. Notice, the scriptures said that God commanded all men to repent (turn from their sinful ways to God).

But the focus will not always be on the whole world. God is, at this time on His calendar, focused on the world and its need to repent. But, eventually, the focus will turn back to the Jewish people. One must understand that all of this is carefully planned by God. The worldwide open door to all mankind will eventually change, and the focus will again return to the Jews.

Isaiah 61:11-62:7 says it this way:

> *For as the earth bringeth forth her bud, and as the garden causeth the things that are sown in it to spring forth; so the Lord God will cause righteousness and praise to spring forth before all the nations. For Zion's sake will I not hold my peace, and for Jerusalem's sake I will not rest, until the righteousness thereof go forth as brightness, and the salvation thereof as a lamp that burneth. And the Gentiles shall see thy righteousness, and all kings thy glory: and thou shalt be called by a new name, which the mouth of the LORD shall name. Thou shalt also be a crown of glory in the hand of the LORD, and a royal diadem in the hand of thy God. Thou shalt no more be termed Forsaken; neither shall thy land any more be termed Desolate: but thou shalt be called Hephzibah, and thy land Beulah: for the LORD delighted in thee, and thy land shall be married. For as a young man marrieth a virgin, so shall thy sons marry thee: and as the bridegroom rejoiceth over the bride, so shall thy God rejoice over thee. I have set watchmen upon thy walls, O Jerusalem, which shall never hold their peace day nor night:*

ye that make mention of the LORD, keep not silence, And give him no rest, till he establish, and till he make Jerusalem a praise in the earth.

God is in charge of all things yet to come. He started with His creation of a people called the Jews, children of Abraham, and used them dramatically. Then He sent His Son to them, and that Son was rejected by the Jews. He then created a Church and sent the Church into the world to invite all those who would become followers of Him to become His chosen people. Therefore, all mankind during this Church age is invited to be a part of God's chosen ones. Since the Jews rejected God, the Gentile world was given a window of opportunity to become His people, but only for a time. This window of invitation to the world is not forever. The door will close and God will turn His attention back to the children of Abraham. The Church age is to be discussed a little later in the book.

Right now let's discuss the kingdom. But keep in mind the questions that began our study:

- **Is there a God?**
- **If so, does He have a reason for creating the people called the Jews?**
- **Is He manipulating the events of the world to serve His purpose?**
- **To what extent has He already determined what has taken place and will take place in this world?**

QUESTION # 10

How did this kingdom, preached by John the Baptist and Jesus, become a part of this plan? Was it a new concept?

The kingdom that was preached by John the Baptist and Jesus Christ was expected and proclaimed many years before they preached about it. It was not a new concept, but when they began to preach it, it marked the arrival of the already prophesied kingdom.

We find references to the eternal kingdom revealed to us in scripture.

Daniel 2:28-45:

> *But there is a God in heaven that revealeth secrets, and maketh known to the king Nebuchadnezzar what shall be in the latter days. Thy dream, and the visions of thy head upon thy bed, are these; As for thee, O king, thy thoughts came into thy mind upon thy bed, what should come to pass hereafter: and he that revealeth secrets maketh known to thee what shall come to pass. But as for me, this secret is not revealed to me for any wisdom that I have more than any living, but for their sakes that shall make known the interpretation to the king, and that thou mightiest know the thoughts of thy heart. Thou, O king, sawest, and behold a great image.*

This great image, whose brightness was excellent, stood before thee; and the form thereof was terrible. This image's head was of fine gold, his breast and his arms of silver, his belly and his thighs of brass, his legs of iron, his feet part of iron and part of clay. Thou sawest till that a stone was cut out without hands, which smote the image upon his feet that were of iron and clay, and brake them to pieces. Then was the iron, the clay, the brass, the silver, and the gold broken to pieces together, and became like the chaff of the summer threshingfloors; and the wind carried them away, that no place was found for them: and the stone that smote the image became a great mountain, and filled the whole earth. This is the dream; and we will tell the interpretation thereof before the king. Thou, O king, art a king of kings: for the God of heaven hath given thee a kingdom, power and strength and glory. And wheresoever the children of men dwell, the beasts of the field and the fowls of the heaven hath he given into thine hand, and hath made thee ruler over them all. Thou art this head of gold. And after thee shall arise another kingdom inferior to thee, and another third kingdom of brass, which shall bear rule over all the earth. And the fourth kingdom shall be strong as iron: forasmuch as iron breaketh in pieces and subdueth all things: and as iron that breaketh all these, shall it break in pieces and bruise. And whereas thou sawest the feet and toes, part of potters' clay, and part of iron, the kingdom shall be divided; but there shall be in it of the strength of the iron, forasmuch as thou sawest the iron mixed with miry clay. And as the toes of the feet were part of iron, and part of clay, so the kingdom shall be partly strong, and partly broken. And whereas thou sawest iron mixed with miry clay, they shall mingle themselves with the seed of men: but they shall not cleave one to another, even as iron is not mixed with clay. And in the days of these kings shall the God of heaven set up a kingdom, which shall never be destroyed: and the kingdom shall not be left to other people, but it shall break in pieces and consume all these kingdoms, and it shall stand forever. Forasmuch as thou sawest that the stone was cut out of the mountain without hands, and that it brake in pieces the iron, the brass, the clay, the silver, and the gold; the great God hath made known to the king what shall come to pass hereafter: and the dream is certain and the interpretation thereof sure.

Looking at the prophecy of Daniel we observe that there will be only four great worldwide empires: Babylon, MedoPersia, Greece and Rome. These were all depicted by the statue in the dream Daniel interpreted for Nebuchadnezzar. The feet that are crushed by the mountain represent the Roman Empire. The mountain was the kingdom of Jesus Christ, and the mountain kingdom will expand into all the world and will never end. This huge stone would represent the kingdom that God created through Christ. Again, let me emphasize: this kingdom will never end.

It is time to answer the question of how this kingdom fits into God's plan. Is this a new idea? We must understand it is not new at all. It was a wonderful thing sent from God and would fill the Earth. It is also important to note that when it began, it would never end. It would go forth and fulfill His purposes.

The King

A kingdom cannot exist without a king. Therefore, there could be no kingdom without Jesus. He is the King that will rule the mountain kingdom.

Isaiah 9:6-7 reveals this: *"For unto us a child is born, unto us a son is given: and the government shall be upon his shoulder: and his name shall be called Wonderful, Counsellor, The mighty God, The everlasting Father, The Prince of Peace. Of the increase of his government and peace there shall be no end, upon the throne of David, and upon his kingdom to order it and to establish it with judgment and with justice from henceforth even for ever. The zeal of the LORD of hosts will perform this."*

These verses not only tell us of the coming of the Prince of Peace, but they also advise us of the kingdom and government that will be established forever. We now know this Prince (Jesus) will sit upon the throne of David.

Kingdom at hand

The King would indeed be born a Prince (child), but would grow to become a King. When Jesus was thirty years old, He then began proclaiming, "The kingdom of Heaven is at hand."

Mark 1:14-15 confirms this, saying, *"Now after that John was put in prison, Jesus came into Galilee, preaching the gospel of the kingdom of God, And saying, The time is fulfilled and the kingdom of God is at hand: repent ye, and believe the gospel."*

When Jesus came into the land of Galilee, He came preaching the KINGDOM OF GOD.

John and Jesus both began preaching the kingdom. It was referred to both as the kingdom of God and the kingdom of Heaven. Some have said that they are one and the same. However, there is an important distinction. The first represents a kingdom that exists as a place (Heaven). The other manifests itself as the person of God.

The kingdom of God is revealed as follows:

Mark 9:1 *"And he said unto them, Verily I say unto you, That there be some of them that stand here, which shall not taste of death till they have seen the kingdom of God come with power."*

Therefore, Jesus ushered in the kingdom while He was reaching out to the Gentiles!

God approached the people of Israel first with the offer of the kingdom. They would reject that gift from God. The offer is accessible to all through the words of John. One might say, they simply did not want the type of kingdom that Jesus was offering. Therefore, God turned and offered it to the Gentiles.

John 3:3 tells us, *"...Except a man be born again, he cannot see the kingdom of God."*

In this verse Jesus is talking to a religious Jewish leader. He tells him that there must be a second birth in order to see the kingdom. Jesus goes on to explain to this man that, just as Moses lifted up the serpent in the wilderness, He must also be lifted up. And in that moment whosoever believeth in Him shall not perish but have eternal life. In order to understand John 3 and the references to the snake, we must return to study the Old Testament reference. In Numbers 21, after Moses led the people of Israel into the wilderness and away from Egypt, they became very disgruntled and God sent snakes upon them to as punishment for their discontent. Moses had to intercede quickly and went before God. He asked God to help him save his people. God told Moses to make a brass snake and then fasten it to a staff. He was to stand before his people holding it upward toward the sky. He told his people to place their trust in God by believing in the sign he held. Those who believed would be unaffected by the bite of the snake. Those who had no faith would die. The comparison here to Genesis cannot be denied. God told Adam to believe in Him and avoid the fruit of the one tree. The snake that contained the poison words of Satan are the snakes threatening the lives of Moses' people. Eve was figuratively bitten by the snake by believing she could gain wisdom. She spread the poison of this message to Adam. They died at that moment in the eyes of God, just as the nonbelievers of Moses' people died. Yet God brought another piece of wood, symbolized in Numbers by Moses' wooden staff, to spare man. He allowed His Son, Jesus, to be fastened to wood so that those who come to believe in Him shall not perish, but have eternal life. However, just as the people of Moses had a choice, so do we. We can only survive Satan's bite by believing in the message of the cross and the death of the Messiah. John 3:3 is our second birth through Christ, which allows us to have salvation. It really is the same as the Cain and Abel story. Cain trusted on his own work, but Abel trusted on the lamb that was slain in order to enjoy the benefits of a righteous walk.

There was a kingdom coming that has no end. It would encompass the entire world. We also know this kingdom was to be born during the time of the Roman Empire. John the Baptist announced the coming of the new kingdom. Then, fulfilling God's prophecy, Jesus paid for the creation of the kingdom with His life. However, since Christ paid a price for us we must pay a price to obtain eternal life. That price is our rebirth and a Christian walk with God. There must be compete devotion. We must give up our life to God as Christ gave up His life for us.

Let's talk more about the King and His arrival!

The Christmas story and its prophetic statements are very important because they proclaim the coming of a Prince – a Prince of Peace. It is about a Prince who would grow up and eventually become King. Isaiah 7:14-16 declares that they would know Him because He would be born of a virgin. Isaiah 9:6-7 says He would be born to have the government on His shoulder, *"and His name shall be called Wonderful, Counsellor, The mighty God, The everlasting Father, The Prince of Peace."* His government will never end. It (the kingdom) will continually increase. Isaiah proclaimed in chapter 11:1-13 that He would be a descendant of Jesse. Jesus proclaimed through His own words that He would come forth and rule the world. In Matthew 19:28, Jesus declared that when He comes in His glory, He shall sit on a throne of glory. In Matthew 25:31 He declares again that He will come with great glory and rule from a throne of glory. Matthew 2:6 says Jesus is declared to be the ruler over the Jews. Mark 10:42 says He shall rule over the Gentiles. Revelation 2:27, 12:5 and 19:15 tell us that He will rule the world with a rod of iron.

It is evident there can be no kingdom without a King.

Zechariah 14:16-17 *"And it shall come to pass, that every one that is left of all the nations which came against Jerusalem shall even go up from year to year to worship the King, the LORD of hosts, and to keep the feasts of tabernacles. And it shall be, that whoso will not come up of all the families of the earth unto Jerusalem to worship the King, the LORD of hosts, even upon them shall be no rain."*

It is clear that the King appointed by God will rule the world in a future day and time. It is also clear that this King will rule the world without anyone able to question His authority.

Revelation 19:16 *"And he hath on his vesture and on his thigh a name written, KING OF KINGS, AND LORD OF LORDS."*

In Revelation 19, we get a look at this coming ruler and His total authority. He will come to take over the leadership of planet Earth.

Matthew 25:34 – *"Then shall the King say unto them on his right hand, Come, ye blessed of my Father, inherit the kingdom prepared for you from the foundation of the world:"*

There is a kingdom coming, and a KING! There is no question as to His identity. If the scripture is researched honestly, one must see the prophecies and the fulfillments of them in the life of Jesus. We do not understand totally how it will be set up or how it will unfold, but it will come. There are only two sides to choose from: those for Christ and those against Him. If you were asked today to which group you belong, what would you say? Are your convictions strong enough to announce to the world that you belong to Christ? Are you living your life as a born-again Christian? Are you sure you have accepted God's gift, or has Satan's snake struck you down? The world is Satan's snake pit. Only you can answer for you!

This moves us to God's Red Carpet Group.

QUESTION # 11

How did the Church become part of God's plan for His world?

How does the Church fit into the kingdom and with the chosen people?

The Church was the special bride of Jesus Christ. The Church was the creation of Jesus Christ.

Matthew 16:13-19:

> *When Jesus came into the coasts of Caesarea Philippi, he asked his disciples, saying, Whom do men say that I the Son of man am? And they said, Some say that thou art John the Baptist: some Elias; and others, Jeremias, or one of the prophets. He saith unto them, But whom say ye that I am? And Simon Peter answered and said, Thou art the Christ, the Son of the living God. And Jesus answered and said unto him, Blessed art thou, Simon Barjona: for flesh and blood hath not revealed it unto thee, but my Father which is in heaven. And I say also unto thee, That thou art Peter, and upon this rock I will build my church; and the gates of hell shall not prevail against it. And I will give unto thee the keys of the kingdom of heaven: and whatsoever thou shalt bind on earth*

shall be bound in heaven: and whatsoever thou shalt loose on earth shall be loosed in heaven.

Jesus required a stronghold to protect His followers. He knew alone they might be weak, but bonded together they would grow stronger. He therefore created the Church (a group of baptized believers). Their purpose was clear – to go into the whole world and tell that Jesus had come to be the sacrificial Lamb of Abel, Abraham, Moses and Aaron, and now for those of us who are born again. But this day of the Church age will not last forever. The Church age is only one phase of God's plan, and it will fade away.

The Church was not an afterthought, but it was not spoken of in the scriptures until Jesus declared it in Matthew. The Church is a very important part of God's plan, but only for an unknown period of time.

The Church is important to Jesus. He referred to it as His "Bride" or His "body." Paul wrote letters to the developing Church to inspire them to grow and share the importance of the Church age.

Ephesians 1:10, 22-23 *"That in the dispensation of the fullness of times he might gather together in one all things in Christ, both which are in heaven, and which are on earth; even in him: (22) And hath put all things under his feet, and gave him to be the head over all things to the church, Which is his body, the fullness of him that filleth all in all."*

Ephesians 2:20-22 *"And are built upon the foundation of the apostles and prophets, Jesus Christ himself being the chief corner stone; In whom all the building fitly framed together groweth unto an holy temple in the Lord: In whom ye also are builded together for an habitation of God through the Spirit."*

Ephesians 5:23-27 *"For the husband is the head of the wife, even as Christ is the head of the Church: and he is the saviour of the body. Therefore as the church is subject unto Christ, so let the wives be to their own husbands in everything. Husbands, love your wives, even as Christ also loved the church, and gave himself for it; That he might sanctify and cleanse it with the washing of water by the word. That he might present it to himself a glorious church, not having spot, or wrinkle, or any such thing; but that it should be holy and without blemish."*

Colossians 1:13, 18 *"Who hath ... translated us into the kingdom of his dear Son ... And he is the head of the body, the church: who is the beginning, the firstborn from the dead; that in all things he might have the preeminence."*

1 Timothy 3:15 *"But if I tarry long, that thou mayest know how thou oughtest to behave thyself in the house of God, which is the church of the living God, the pillar and ground of the truth."*

The Church is the living body of the Spirit of Christ. It is therefore the home of God through His Holy Spirit. It is a wonderful creation of Jesus to be gloriously held up as a gift for the Father. God shows us the importance of His Church by telling us about it in the following verses:

- Created by Jesus Himself – Matthew 16:17-19
- Added to by the invitation of the Holy Spirit and consecrated to Him by baptism – Acts 2:47
- Commissioned to be fed – Acts 20:28

- Given its earthly focus and calling – Matthew 28:18-20 and Acts 1:8
- In houses at first – Romans 16:5 and 1 Corinthians 16:19
- To be presented glorious in the future – Ephesians 5:27
- For His body's sake – Colossians 1:24
- To be the Church of the firstborn – Hebrews 12:23
- John wrote to the seven Churches – Revelation 2 and 3
- The Church is the New Jerusalem – Revelation 21:2
- Testify these things in the Churches – Revelation 22:16

The kingdom is proclaimed all over the Old Testament. It was proclaimed by the prophets. The King is coming and the kingdom will be built. This King will eventually rule the world from the throne of Jerusalem. These truths are revealed to us as we walk through the Old and New Testaments. It is clear that God had as an element of His plan, to have a bride called the Church.

As God's bride, the Church has a purpose on Earth. It has a limited time on Earth, but will reign for an eternity with Him.

The King, the kingdom, and the Church are all part of God's plan for the ages. We are in the Church age at present, which is a part of the kingdom. Are you a part of the Church and, in turn, a part of the kingdom?

The Church is the group responsible for rolling out the red (blood-paved) carpet for the world. It is God's intention to send the Church into all the world proclaiming the offer to mankind to become reunited with their Creator. It can only be achieved through trusting in the sacrifice of the Lamb, Jesus Christ.

The Church is God's 911 team sent to rescue the dying human race, one at a time.

Matthew 28:18-20 *"And Jesus came and spake unto them, saying, All power is given unto me in heaven and in earth. Go ye therefore, and teach all nations, baptizing them in the name of the Father, and of the Son, and of the Holy Ghost. Teaching them to observe all things whatsoever I have commanded you: and, lo, I am with you alway, even unto the end of the world. Amen."*

We who are His Church have work to do. This is why I am writing this, and why you are reading it.

Now we must move back to the subject of the Jews, which leads us to the next question.

QUESTION # 12

What happens to the Jews during the Church age?

It cannot be emphasized enough that God sought after Israel first to be His bride. But they rejected Him. This, however, did not prohibit the Jewish people from becoming believers and born-again members of the Church that Jesus built. They were and are as welcome as any other group of people. The Church age is the time when God is stretching His arms out to every man, woman, boy and girl in the world. It is the time of the earthly invitation. But the worldwide invitation will not last forever. There is a distinct time frame in God's plan called the Church age. The words of Jesus, in Matthew 16:18, tell us, *"Upon this rock I will build my church: and the gates of hell shall not prevail against it."* These words tell us that Jesus would build the Church Himself and that it would be a force against which all of Hell could not prevail.

It is quite clear that the Church age will only last for a finite period on the planet. The Church is the vehicle God uses to invite the world to come and be a unified people unto Him. The Church age has ushered in a worldwide invitation to preach the gospel of Jesus Christ. The

Church is to bring to life the story of the Messiah. It is to tell of a sinless life followed by a sacrificial death and, finally, the resurrection of the body. This message is to herald the return of Christ the King to His throne in Jerusalem for a finite period. After this time, Christ will return to Heaven for eternity.

This is the mission of the Church. But the Church, according to scripture, will soon disappear from God's earthly activities. From chapters four through nine, the word "Church" does not appear. 1 Corinthians 15:51-53 tells us, *"Behold, I shew you a mystery; We shall not all sleep, but we shall be changed, In a moment, in the twinkling of an eye, at the last trump: for the trumpet shall sound, and the dead shall be raised incorruptible, and we shall be changed. For this corruptible must put on incorruption, and this mortal must put on immortality."*

1 Thessalonians 4:13-18 *"But I would not have you to be ignorant, brethren, concerning them which are asleep, that ye sorrow not, even as others which have no hope. For if we believe that Jesus died and rose again, even so them also which sleep in Jesus will God bring with Him. For this we say unto you by the word of the Lord, that we which are alive and remain unto the coming of the Lord shall not prevent them which are asleep. For the Lord himself shall descend from heaven with a shout, with the voice of the archangel, and with the trump of God: and the dead in Christ shall rise first: Then we which are alive and remain shall be caught up together with them in the clouds to meet the Lord in the air: and so shall we ever be with the Lord. Wherefore comfort one another with these words."* This passage tells us that God will soon

bring the Church age to a close. There are many Bible scholars who believe God will protect His Church. They believe that God will provide a veil of protection so that His Church will survive. God has established historical precedent for this. The protection of Noah from the flood and the removal of Lot from Sodom and Gomorrah are prime examples of God's protection. There are those who take comfort in the idea that the born-again Christian will be spared God's wrath as the Church age comes to a close. There are many differing opinions about the destiny of the Church. But what seems apparent is that, when we compare events at the end of the world to other biblical events, the Church age will come to be known as the invitational period. After the Church age passes, God's invitational period to know Him will be offered back to the seed of Abraham. Then Jesus will come to rule the world.

Revelation 5-18 is focused totally around the nation of Israel and its people. The last plagues are experienced worldwide, but their main focus is on and around Jerusalem. These events are referred to in scripture as "The Day of Jacob's Trouble." God will accept repentance from Gentiles as He did with Hagar and Ruth, for example, in the Old Testament. His focus, however, is primarily on the Jews. God tells us in Revelation that a dictator shall arise to persecute the Jewish people. Those who will not comply will suffer death. Revelation 14:1-5 tells that 144,000 Jewish ministers will spread God's Word to the Jews. God also describes to us in Revelation 11 that two bold prophets will come and preach to the Jews in Jerusalem only to be killed in the streets by the nonbelievers. Both of these events will take place while the evil dictator is in charge of the world.

God will purge the Jewish people

There is much confusion about how these last days of the Church age, as well as "The Day of Jacob's Trouble" will unfold. But one thing is clear – according to the book of Revelation, when the Church age is over, the world will be in a state of doom. The Jews who have rejected God's invitation during the Old Testament age and the Church age will be in confusion, and great wrath will come.

However, Israel will be protected by God and preserved for future purposes. They will suffer greatly because of their rejections, but God still has a future for them. During the Church age, God will begin to draw them back together as a nation. Scripture teaches us that at the end of the Church age, there will be a regathering and a purging of the Jews as a nation.

Matthew 24:15-31:

> *When ye therefore shall see the abomination of desolation, spoken of by Daniel the prophet, stand in the holy place, (whoso readeth, let him understand:) Then let them which be in Judaea flee into the mountains: Let him which is on the housetop not come down to take any thing out of his house: Neither let him which is in the field return back to take his clothes. And woe unto them that are with child, and to them that give suck in those days! But pray ye that your flight be not in the winter, neither on the sabbath day: For then*

shall be great tribulation, such as was not since the beginning of the world to this time, no, nor ever shall be. And except those days should be shortened, there should no flesh be saved: but for the elect's sake those days shall be shortened. Then if any man shall say unto you lo, here is Christ, or there: believe it not. For there shall arise false Christs, and false prophets, and shall shew great signs and wonders; insomuch that, if it were possible, they shall deceive the very elect. Behold, I have told you before. Wherefore if they shall say unto you, Behold he is in the desert; go not forth: behold, he is in the secret chambers; believe it not. For as the lightning cometh out of the east, and shineth even unto the west; so shall also the coming of the Son of man be. For wheresoever the carcase is, there will the eagles be gathered together. Immediately after the tribulation of those days shall the sun be darkened, and the moon shall not give her light, and the stars shall fall from heaven, and the powers of the heavens shall be shaken: And then shall appear the sign of the Son of man in heaven: and then shall all the tribes of the earth morn, and they shall see the Son of man coming in the clouds of heaven with great power and great glory. And he shall send his angels with a great sound of a trumpet, and they shall gather together his elect from the four winds, from one end of heaven to the other.

Jesus made many bold claims of how the future was in the hands of God and how He (God) was going to bring the history of this planet to a close at His direction. It is also clear that the people of Judea would have a bold part in the last days of this planet's history. The abomination of desolation is a reference to the prophecy of Daniel. Daniel prophesied that there would be a world leader who would rule the world during this time of Jacob's trouble. This ruler would make a peace agreement with the nation of Israel for a short time. Then this ruler would break the agreement and lead the world into false worship of him. The Jews will refuse, and this ruler will take over the newly built temple in Jerusalem. He will build a statue of himself in the temple and command all to worship it. This is what is known as the "abomination of desolation."

Matthew 24 records the event in a sermon preached by Jesus. Jesus tells us the Jewish people will see this event take place. Jesus instructs them to go into the hills to hide. This event signifies the coming of great trials and tribulations. As He did Noah and Lot, He seeks to shield His people from the results of this idolatry. He tells the Jewish people the signs they must watch for in order to avoid persecution. God was always looking to protect those who listened to Him.

God will preserve the Jewish people

Revelation 12:1-11

> *And there appeared a great wonder in heaven; a woman clothed with the sun, and the moon under her feet, upon her head a crown of twelve stars: And she being with child cried, travailing in birth, and pained to be delivered. And there appeared another wonder in heaven; and behold a great red dragon, having seven heads and ten horns, and*

seven crowns upon his heads. And his tail drew the third part of the stars of heaven, and did cast them to the earth: and the dragon stood before the woman which was ready to be delivered, for to devour her child as soon as it was born. And she brought forth a man child, who was to rule all nations with a rod of iron: and her child was caught up unto God, and to his throne. And the woman fled into the wilderness, where she hath a place prepared of God, that they should feed her there a thousand two hundred and threescore days. And there was war in heaven: Michael and his angels fought against the dragon; and the dragon fought and his angels, And prevailed not; neither was their place found any more in heaven. And the great dragon was cast out, that old serpent, called the Devil, and Satan, which deceiveth the whole world: he was cast out into the earth, and his angels were cast out with him. And I heard a loud voice saying in heaven, Now is come salvation, and strength, and the kingdom of our God, and the power of his Christ: for the accuser of our brethren is cast down, which accused them before our God day and night. And they overcame him by the blood of the Lamb, and by the word of their testimony; and they loved not their lives unto the death.

In Revelation 12:1-10, God is giving us an overhead look at God's people (the woman being with child). She delivered the Christ Child, who will rule with a rod of iron. Satan tried to kill the Child, but failed. The woman was ushered into the wilderness to protect her for a time.

This passage of scripture is not easily understood. It has been and still is a mystery. We understand who she is because we have the rest of the Bible to explain this passage. We understand who the Child is because of the description of Him. But today we simply know by this passage that God protected the woman (the nation of Israel) and will protect her for His purposes past, present and future.

God is going to protect the children of Abraham for the days ahead. It is clear through prophecy that God scattered the Israelite people all over the world as a result of their rejection of Jesus. They were scattered for many years until He had accomplished His purposes for the Gentiles. Then the Jews would be regathered to fulfill their purpose. God means for us to see this as the repurchasing of Gomer in the later days of her life. Just as Gomer rejected Hosea's love, Israel rejected God's love. Just as Gomer did not appreciate Hosea's special relationship, Israel did not appreciate God's special blessings. Therefore, just as Hosea let her go to her lovers, God let Israel go to her lovers. And just as Hosea purchased Gomer back at the end of her life, God will purchase the nation of Israel back at the end of life on Earth.

As we have seen, God introduced the day of the Gentiles. However, the heart of God is proclaimed in many prophecies.

Those prophecies proclaim that God has a heart for Israel just as Hosea had a heart for Gomer!

God regathers His Jewish people

The regathering for the last days of Earth's life is clearly proclaimed in the prophecies of Israel. Ezekiel 37 – The dry bones chapter remains a confusing scripture to many people.

Ezekiel 37:1-14:

> *The hand of the Lord was upon me, and carried me out in the spirit of the LORD, and set me down in the midst of the valley which was full of bones, And caused me to pass by them round about: and behold, there were very many in the open valley; and, lo, they were very dry. And he said unto me, Son of man, can these bones live? And I answered, O LORD GOD, thou knowest. Again he said unto me, Prophesy upon these bones, and say unto them, O ye dry bones, hear the word of the LORD. Thus saith the LORD God unto these bones, Behold I will cause breath to enter into you, and ye shall live. And I will lay sinews upon you, and will bring up flesh upon you, and cover you with skin, and put breath in you, and ye shall live; and ye shall know that I am the LORD. So I prophesied as I was commanded: and as I prophesied, there was a noise, and behold a shaking, and the bones came together, bone to his bone. And when I beheld, lo the sinews and the flesh came up upon them, and the skin covered them above: but there was no breath in them. Then said he unto me, Prophecy unto the wind, prophesy, son of man, and say to the wind, thus saith the Lord GOD; Come from the four winds, O breath, and breathe upon these slain,*

that they may live. So I prophesied as he commanded me, and the breath came into them, and they lived, and stood up upon their feet, an exceeding great army. Then he said unto me, Son of man, these bones are the whole house of Israel: behold, they say, Our bones are dried, and our hope is lost: we are cut off for our parts. Therefore prophesy and say unto them, Thus saith the Lord God; Behold, O my people, I will open your graves, and cause you to come up out of your graves, and bring you into the land of Israel. And ye shall know that I am the LORD, when I have opened your graves, O my people, and brought you up out of your graves, And shall put my spirit in you, and ye shall live, and I shall place you in your own land: then shall ye know that I the LORD have spoken it, and performed it, saith the LORD.

The prophecy of the valley of dry bones has been misunderstood for many years. The valley of dry bones represents the dead nation of Israel. God poses the question to Ezekiel, "Can these bones live?" Then God tells Ezekiel that they will live. God says that the wind of the spirit will bring them to life. In verse 12 God tells the people of Israel that He will bring them from the graves piece by piece. He tells them that He will bring them into the land of Israel, and that He will put His spirit into them and they shall live. God then assures them that He will place them in their own land. In this way, the Jews would know that the LORD has spoken.

It is clear, that if the Jews are to be brought together, they must first be scattered at large. They were scattered after the destruction of the temple in 70 A.D., and since 1947 the Jewish people have been miraculously returning to Israel daily. In 2004 it was said that one-half of all the Jewish people on the planet were living in the land of Israel, and more are returning each day. This is why Israel has many controversial Jewish settlements. They are needed as the Jews look to return to their true home as prophesied by God.

The fulfillment of Ezekiel is unraveling in front of our very eyes. If we are willing to watch for the signs God is revealing to us, we can clearly see that He is real and involved in the events of the Earth.

Isaiah defines a time when the Jews are dependent on the Gentiles.

Isaiah 61:1-62:2

> *The Spirit of the Lord God is upon me; because the LORD hath anointed me to preach good tidings unto the meek; he hath sent me to bind up the broken hearted, to proclaim liberty to the captives, and the opening of the prison to them that are bound; To proclaim the acceptable year of the LORD, and the day of vengeance of our God; to comfort all that mourn; To appoint unto them that mourn in Zion, to give unto them beauty for ashes, the oil of joy for mourning, the garment of praise for the spirit of heaviness; that they might be called trees of righteousness, the planting of the LORD, that he might be glorified. And they shall build the old wastes, they shall raise up the former desolations, and they shall repair the waste cities,*

the desolations of many generations. And strangers shall stand and feed your flocks, and the sons of the alien shall be your plowmen and your vinedressers. But ye shall be named the Priests of the LORD; men shall call you the Ministers of our God: ye shall eat the riches of the Gentiles, and in their glory shall ye boast yourselves. For your shame ye shall have double; and for confusion they shall rejoice in their portion: therefore in their land they shall possess the double: everlasting joy shall be unto them. For I the LORD love judgment, I hate robbery for burnt offering: and I will direct their work in truth, and I will make an everlasting covenant with them. And their seed shall be known among the Gentiles, and their offspring among the people: all that see them shall acknowledge them, that they are the seed which the Lord hath blessed. I will greatly rejoice in the LORD, my soul shall be joyful in my God; for he hath clothed me with the garments of salvation, he hath covered me with the robe of righteousness, as a bridegroom decketh himself with ornaments, and as a bride adorneth herself with her jewels. For as the earth bringeth forth her bud, and as the garden causeth the things that are sown in it to spring forth; so the Lord God will cause righteousness and praise to spring forth before all the nations. For Zion's sake will I not hold my peace, and for Jerusalem's sake I will not rest, until the righteousness thereof go forth as brightness, and the salvation thereof as a lamp that burneth. And the Gentiles shall see thy righteousness, and all kings the glory: and thou

> *shalt be called by a new name, which the mouth of the LORD shall name. Thou shalt also be a crown of glory in the hand of the LORD, and a royal diadem in the hand of thy God.*

It is apparent that God told the Jewish people through Isaiah the prophet that they would be scattered because of their rejection. He tells them that they will be regathered to rebuild the old wastes. He also says that because of the confusion of the Jews and rejection of God, the Gentiles will be blessed. He says that all Gentiles will be blessed, but that there will be a particular Gentile nation that will stand out as being the most blessed nation. That nation will be acknowledged as one that has an everlasting covenant with God, and that God has blessed above all others. One might hope this might be the United States of America. No other nation in history has ever fit this description like America. Some would argue that this is the Medo-Persian Empire as Isaiah wrote about it before it was taken away by the Babylonians. But the Medo-Persian Empire does not fit this description. Let me give you a few words that will describe the relationship Isaiah said would be a part of that nation. Verse 6 says, *"Ye shall eat the riches of the Gentiles, and, in their glory shall you boast yourself,"* and verse 7 says, *"For your shame ye shall have double and for confusion they shall rejoice in their portion, therefore in their land they shall possess the double: everlasting joy shall be unto them."* Verse 8 says, *"... I will direct their work in truth, I will make an everlasting covenant with them,"* and verse 9 says, *"And their seed shall be known among the Gentiles and their offspring among the people: all that see them shall acknowledge them, that they are the seed the which the LORD hath blessed."*

What evidence do we have that supports America as God's special haven of the Gentiles? If one studies the beginnings of America, our history proclaims that America was discovered, founded, formed and freed by the hand of God. America has been blessed above all nations by God's grace. The Medes and the Persians have not received an everlasting covenant with God.

America is blessing Israel and Israel is being regathered. Note verse 11: God's declaration regarding this prophecy being fulfilled – *"...The LORD God will cause righteousness and praise to spring forth before all the nations."*

It is exciting to see the hand of God and to be a part of it. The fact that you have chosen to read this book is a proclamation of verse 11: *"For as the earth bringeth forth her bud, and as the garden causeth the things that are sown in it to spring forth; so the Lord God will cause righteousness and praise to spring forth before all the nations."*

Jeremiah 16 – Coming back from the north

Jeremiah 16:14:

> *Therefore, behold, the days come, saith the LORD, that it shall not more be said, The LORD liveth, that brought up the children of Israel out of the land of Egypt; But, the LORD liveth, that brought up the children of Israel out of the land of the north, and from all the lands wither he had driven*

them: and I will bring them again into their land that I gave unto their fathers. Behold, I will send for many fishers, saith the LORD, and they shall fish them; and after will I send for many hunters, and they shall hunt them from every mountain, and from every hill, and out of the holes of the rocks. For mine eyes are upon all their ways: they are not hid from my face, neither is their iniquity hid from mine eyes. And first I will recompense their iniquity and their sin double; because they have defiled my land, they have filled mine inheritance with the carcases of their detestable and abominable things. O LORD, my strength, and my fortress, and my refuge in the day of affliction, the Gentiles shall come unto thee from the ends of the earth, and shall say, Surely our fathers have inherited lies, vanity, and things wherein there is no profit. Shall a man make gods unto himself, and they are not gods? Therefore, behold, I will this once cause them to know, I will cause them to know mine hand and my might; and they shall know that my name is The LORD.

Three things:

1. Coming from Egypt will be an old story.
2. Coming home from the land of the north will be the story.
3. The Gentiles will only get one opportunity to experience Jehovah God.

These three thing are distinct, and we are experiencing them even today. During the Ronald Reagan presidency, the fall of Communism was the big story. With the fall of

Communism came an opportunity for the Jewish people to leave Russia, which is the land directly north of the land of Israel. There were television commercials that ran asking people to send money to help a Jewish person leave Russia. We were asked to help them return to their native Israel. They had been exiled there for generations, and this was the time to help them go home.

This happened during the Gentile age – the age of the invitation to come and get to know Jehovah God through knowing Jesus Christ.

Jeremiah 23:1-8 – The promised return of the remnant

Jeremiah 23:1-8:

> *Woe be unto the pastors that destroy and scatter the sheep on my pasture! Saith the LORD. Therefore thus saith the LORD God of Israel against the pastors that feed my people; Ye have scattered my flock, and driven them away, and have not visited them: behold, I will visit upon you the evil of your doings, saith the LORD. And I will gather the remnant of my flock out of all countries whither I have driven them, and will bring them again to their folds; and they shall be fruitful and increase. And I will set up shepherds over them which shall feed them: and they shall fear no more, nor be dismayed, neither shall they be lacking, saith the LORD. Behold, the days come, saith the LORD, that I will raise unto David a righteous Branch, and a King shall reign and prosper, and shall execute judgment and justice in the earth. In*

> *his days Judah shall be saved, and Israel shall dwell safely: and this is his name whereby he shall be called, THE LORD OUR RIGHTEOUSNESS. Therefore, behold, the days come, saith the LORD, that they shall no more say, the LORD liveth, which brought up the children of Israel out of the land of Egypt: But, the LORD liveth, which brought up and which led the seed of the house of Israel out of the north country, and from all countries wither I had driven them; and they shall dwell in their own land.*

God is declaring here in Jeremiah that He will bring forth a King Who will rule on the Earth. He also assures us that Judah shall be saved and dwell safely. His name shall be THE LORD OUR RIGHTEOUSNESS. He also declares that He will bring them back to the land of Israel from every nation where they have been scattered.

Because of the rejection of both God and Jesus by the Jewish nation, they were scattered to the ends of the Earth. God had come to Israel first and invited them to become His bride, but was rejected. While the Jews were exiled from their land, God turned to the Gentiles to offer them salvation. The final mark of God will be to bring His chosen people back into His flock and to lead them as the good shepherd. This will be the final chapter of God's book for the nation of Israel.

Jesus was continually beset by Jewish leaders who challenged His words and His God-given authority. Matthew records one of these episodes in chapters 21 and 22. Jesus cleansed the temple of the moneychangers, and this brought on a confrontation that propelled Jesus into a sermon. While preaching to these misguided Pharisees, Jesus told parable after parable declaring that man cannot enter into the kingdom of Heaven by natural progression. He told of an unfruitful fig tree that was cut down because of its lack of fruit. He told of two sons who were called to work with their father. One son told his father that he would work. However, he did not work. His other son, a sinner, repented of his evil ways and began to work. Jesus told another parable of a wicked land tenant left in charge by the landowner. When asked for the profits coming to him, the tenant (husbandman) abused the messengers and even killed the son of the owner. Then Jesus related this story to them and said in Matthew 21:43, *"Therefore say I unto you, The kingdom of God shall be taken from you, and given to a nation bringing forth the fruits thereof."*

Then in chapter 21:45-22:10, Jesus told this story:

> *And when the chief priests and Pharisees had heard his parables, they perceived that he spake of them. But when they sought to lay hands on him they feared the multitude, because they took him for a prophet. And Jesus answered and spake unto them again by parables and said, The kingdom of heaven is like unto a certain king, which made a marriage for his son. And sent forth his servants to call them that were bidden to the wedding and they would not come. Again, he sent forth other servants, saying, Tell them which are bidden, Behold, I have prepared my dinner: my oxen and my fatlings are killed, and all things are ready: come unto the marriage. But they made light of it, and went their ways, one to his farm, another to his*

merchandise: And the remnant took his servants, and entreated them spitefully, and slew them, But when the king heard thereof, he was wroth: and he sent forth his armies and destroyed those murderers, and burned up their city. Then saith he to his servants, The wedding is ready, but they which were bidden were not worthy. Go ye therefore into the highways, and as many as ye shall find, bid to the marriage. So those servants went out into the highways, and gathered together all as many as they found, both bad and good: and the wedding was furnished with guests.

What we know from reading in the Old Testament prophets and the words of Jesus is that, because of this rejection of Jesus and His father, the Gentiles would be a part of the wedding celebration.

God's people become a worldwide irritation

History has continually shown us that the Jews are often at odds with the rest of the world. God has established a conflict between the Jews and all other nations with few exceptions. It is clear by the prophesies concerning them that God has allowed this hardship, whether it is for their punishment or for His purpose.

Let's examine the prophet Zechariah's declaration of the Jews' days of trouble.

Zechariah 12 – Jerusalem's burdensome stone

Zechariah 12:1-9

The burden of the word of the LORD for Israel, saith the LORD, which stretcheth forth the heavens, and layeth the foundation of the earth, and formeth the spirit of man within him. Behold, I will make Jerusalem a cup of trembling unto all the people round about, when they shall be in the siege both against Judah and against Jerusalem. And in that day will I make Jerusalem a burdensome stone for all people: all that burden themselves with it shall be cut in pieces, though all the people of the earth be gathered together against it. In that day, saith the LORD, I will smite every horse with astonishment, and his rider with madness: and I will open mine eyes upon the house of Judah, and will smith every horse of the people with blindness. And the governors of Judah shall say in their heart, The inhabitants of Jerusalem shall be my strength in the LORD of hosts their God. In that day will I make the governors of Judah like an hearth of fire among the wood, and like a torch of fire in a sheaf; and they shall devour all the people round about, on the right hand and on the left: and Jerusalem shall be inhabited again in her own place, even in Jerusalem. The LORD also shall save the tents of Judah first, that the glory of the house of David and the glory of the inhabitants of Jerusalem do not magnify themselves against Judah. In that day shall the LORD defend the inhabitants of Jerusalem; and he

> *that is feeble among them at that day shall be as David; and the house of Davis shall be as God, as the angel of the LORD before them And it shall come to pass in that day, that I will seek to destroy all the nations that come against Jerusalem.*

A word study will show that the phrase "in that day" is continually repeated in the Old and New Testaments. This specific phrase points to a day when everything will be put under the power of the Son of God. He will then return everything to its proper order. This reference is used when speaking of the return of Christ to save the world from decay and ruin. There will be an appointed rescue planned and performed when the whole world unites against the nation of Israel. The climax of the phases, a cup of trembling and a burdensome stone, will then come to its peak, and God will send the King to defend them. The Old and New Testaments call it "in or on that day."

Other prophets have described this attack, and even listed some of the attackers!

Yes, the Jews who are scattered all over are being regathered now from the four corners of the world, but especially from the land of the north.

Remember our questions:

- **Is there a God?**
- **If so, does He have a reason for creating the people called the Jews?**
- **Is He manipulating the events of the world to serve His purpose?**
- **To what extent has He already determined what has taken place and will take place in this world?**

QUESTION # 13

How does the Church age come to a close?

It is a mystery just how the Church age will come to a close, but it is clear that it will happen. There are many scriptures that point to a removal of the Church. At the end of the Church age, God will sound a trumpet and the dead in Christ will rise first. Then we who are alive and remain will be caught up to meet the Lord in the air, and so shall we ever be with the Lord. This is a statement made by the Apostle Paul in 1 Thessalonians 4:13-18. Paul goes on to say in 1 Thessalonians 5 that when this coming takes place we know not, but we do know it will be like a thief in the night. In 1 Corinthians 15:51, Paul also introduces a mystery of the great stealing away and a change that will take place as the Church goes up to meet the Lord in the air. Note, they are going up to meet Him (Christ) in the air. It seems that the Church is taken away from the Earth for a time. One might study the scriptures relating to the removal of the Church and surmise that they are taken away before the purging and final gathering of the Jews. It is unclear in scripture just how and when this calling away will take place. It is clear, however, that it will happen. This is clearly a different time than that of the return of the Lord of lords and King of kings that will come in the book of Revelation chapter 19.

The Church age will come to a close, and it will be a surprise.

After the end of the Church age, scriptures teach that there will be a time of trouble like this world has never seen.

Matthew 24:15-21

> *When ye therefore shall see the abomination of desolation, spoken of by Daniel the prophet, stand in the holy place, (whoso readeth, let him understand:) Then let them which be in Judaea flee into the mountains: Let him which is on the housetop not come down to take any thing out of his house: Neither let him which is in the field return back to take his clothes. And woe unto them that are with child, and to them that give suck in those days! But pray ye that your flight be not in the winter, neither on the sabbath day: For then shall be great tribulation, such as was not since the beginning of the world to this time, no, nor ever shall be.*

Jesus predicted the trouble ahead. It is important to note Jesus teaches this to the Jews. He does so preparing them for the fact that they will be at the center of this turmoil. We must also point out that the Jewish people are in their homeland when this takes place. The people of Israel are the point of this scripture. The reference to the "abomination of desolation" is a term used by Daniel the prophet to explain the coming of these troubling days for the Jewish people.

Jesus goes on in His teaching in Matthew 24:29-31:

> *Immediately after the tribulation of those days shall the sun be darkened, and the moon shall not give her light, and the stars shall fall from heaven, and the powers of the heavens shall be shaken: And then shall appear the sign of the Son of man in heaven: and then shall all the tribes of the earth morn, and they shall see the Son of man coming in the clouds of heaven with great power and great glory. And he shall send his angels with a great sound of a trumpet, and they shall gather together his elect from the four winds, from one end of heaven to the other.*

Scripture reveals that these times of turmoil are "The Day of Jacob's Trouble." It is during this time that Jesus will appear to rule the world. He will rule Heaven and Earth. The account of Jesus' trial tells us much more about the future. During the trial of Jesus by the Jewish rulers, Christ foretells of this event just prior to His crucifixion. Mark 14:62 says, *"And Jesus said, I am: and ye shall see the Son of man sitting on the right hand of power, and coming in the clouds of heaven."*

The days of trouble will come to a close with Jesus returning to deliver the world from the terrible devastation caused by the many plagues and judgments of the tribulation of those days. A "man of sin" will come, and he will try to rule the world. He is called the Antichrist. He will be the one world dictator who will take over the world, empowered by the devil. He is the one who will commit the act of abomination that will bring destruction in the temple in Jerusalem. There will be an image of himself, standing in the temple. People will be forced to worship his graven image, which will mark the end of the tribulation and the coming of the real King of kings and Lord of lords.

Ezekiel 38-39 – Gog and Magog

Ezekiel 38:14 – 39:8

> *Therefore, son of man, prophesy and say unto Gog, Thus saith the Lord GOD; In that day when my people of Israel dwelleth safely, shalt thou not know it? And thou shalt come from thy place out of the north parts, thou and many people with thee, all of them riding upon horses, a great company and a mighty army: And thou shalt come up against my people of Israel, as a cloud to cover the land; it shall be in the latter days, and I will bring thee against my land, that the heathen may know me, when I shall be sanctified in thee, O Gog, before their eyes. Thus saith the Lord GOD; Art thou he of whom I have spoken in old time by my servants the prophets of Israel, which prophesied in those days many years that I would bring thee against them? And it shall come to pass at the same time when Gog shall come against the land of Israel, saith the Lord GOD, that my fury shall come up in my face. For in my jealousy and in the first of my wrath have I spoken, Surely in that day there shall be a great shaking in the land of Israel; So that the fishes of the sea and the fowls of the heaven, and the beasts of the field, and all creeping things that creep upon the earth, and all the men that are upon the face of the earth, shall shake at my presence, and the mountains shall be thrown*

down, and the steep places shall fall, and every wall shall fall to the ground. And I will call for a sword against him throughout all my mountains, saith the Lord GOD: every man's sword shall be against his brother. And I will plead against him with pestilence and with blood; and I will rain upon him, and upon his bands, and upon the many people that are with him, an overflowing rain, and great hailstones, fire, and brimstone. Thus will I magnify myself, and sanctify myself, and I will be known in the eyes of many nations, and they shall know that I am the LORD. Therefore, thou son of man, prophesy against Gog, and say, Thus saith the Lord GOD; Behold, I am against thee, O Gog, the chief prince of Meshech and Tubal: And I will turn thee back, and leave but the sixth part of thee, and will cause thee to come up from the north parts, and will bring thee upon the mountains of Israel: And I will smith thy bow out of thy left hand, and will cause thine arrows to fall out of thy right hand. Thou shalt fall upon the mountains of Israel, thou, and all thy bands, and the people that is with thee: I will give thee unto the ravenous birds of every sort, and to the beasts of the field to be devoured. Thou shalt fall upon the open field: for I have spoken it, saith the Lord GOD. And I will send a fire on Magog, and among them that dwell carelessly in the isles: and they shall know that I am the LORD. So will I make my holy name known in the midst of my people Israel; and I will not let them pollute my holy name any more: and the heathen shall know that I am the LORD, the Holy

One of Israel. Behold it is come, and it is done, saith the Lord GOD; this is the day whereof I have spoken.

Ezekiel makes this even more clear to us. He reveals that while dwelling in their land safely, they will be hated. It is important to note that a prominent religion of Russia today is Islam. It is Gog and Magog (ancient cities existing as Russia today) who will hate Israel and therefore decide to march on Israel to destroy it. Then God will return with swift judgment on Gog and Magog. He will rescue His bride from certain destruction. It is readily apparent from today's events why they would wish to attack Israel. They believe the same as the Islamic neighbors of Israel who have but one desire – destroy her. It seems it is God's plan to eventually use this hatred to destroy the Islamic nations. It will be the final chapter of God's purpose for the conflict of Israel.

1. The northern cities of Gog and Magog (which are ancient cities in Russia) will invade the land of Israel.
2. God will defend Israel Himself.
3. The holy name of God will be declared to Israel and the rest of the world.

Revelation 6:12 – The River Euphrates dries

Revelation 16:12 *"And the sixth angel poured out his vial upon the great river Euphrates; and the water thereof was dried up, that the way of the kings of the east might be prepared."*

Revelation 16:16 *"And he gathered them together into a place called in the Hebrew tongue Armageddon."*

Revelation 19:19 *"And I saw the beast and the kings of the earth, and their armies, gathered together to make war against him that sat on the horse, and against his army."*

They are coming!

The enemies of the world will come to assault Israel and the Master will come and defend them. Zechariah 12 tells us that Jerusalem will be attacked because it is a burdensome stone, and God will give Israel's governors miraculous abilities to fight them with fire. Finally, the angel of the Lord will come before them. Ezekiel says that the northerners will come against them. This will result in God turning the elements of nature against them to devour them. And in the book of Revelation, we are told that the river Euphrates will be dried up and the kings from the east will come and gather in the valley called Armageddon. This will usher in the final judgments on the Earth just before God ushers in His final thousand-year reign.

We do not know every detail that leads up to the end of life on Earth as we know it. We are told that the nation of Israel will be at the center of the battle. The hatred of the world for them will continue to grow until the whole world seems to be united in an effort to destroy Israel, and then God will come forth in power and great glory to rescue His beloved people. Then the Christ (the Anointed One) will come in power and great glory. This will herald the onset of the reign of Christ over the world. That is when the world will experience peace brought on by the Prince of Peace. Then Christ will rule the world with a rod of iron for a thousand years.

Let me ask you:

- **Is there a God?**
- **If so, does He have a reason for creating the people called the Jews?**
- **Is He manipulating the events of the world to serve His purpose?**
- **To what extent has He already determined what has taken place and will take place in this world?**

This leads us to the next question!

QUESTION # 14

What is Armageddon?

Megiddo means "troops."

Armageddon means "many troops."

The battle of Armageddon will be the greatest battle on Planet Earth. They will unite from many directions. Their battleground will be in the valley of Megiddo. This battle will be fought to rescue the Earth from the wicked. The victory will belong to the King of kings and Lord of lords. Then God's story, from Abraham to Armageddon will be complete.

In Revelation 4:1, Heaven opens to let the Church in. But here Heaven opens to let Christ and His armies ride out of Heaven to victory over the forces of evil that have united against the Jewish people.

It is important to understand and acknowledge that presently the world shows this event beginning to take shape. Nations have already begun to unite.

Christ said that He would ride forth and ride to conquer. He was abandoned by His followers in His hour of trouble, but He will come to deliver the Jews in their hour of trouble. Christ will come with a host of angels. He could have called out to these angels to prevent His death on the cross, but Christ appreciated His Father's plan for the salvation of His people. He therefore took upon His shoulders the weight of all the Jews and Gentiles to salvage them, fulfilling the prophecy of His Father.

Zechariah 14 give details of the rescue:

Zechariah 14:1-21:

> *Behold, the day of the LORD cometh, and thy spoil shall be divided in the midst of thee. For I will gather all nations against Jerusalem to battle; and the city shall be taken, and the houses rifled, and the women ravished; and half of the city shall go forth into captivity, and the residue of the people shall not be cut off from the city. Then shall the LORD go forth, and fight against those nations, as when he fought in the day of battle. And his feet shall stand in that day upon the mount of Olives, which is before Jerusalem on the east, and the mount of Olives shall cleave in the midst thereof toward the east and toward the west, and there shall be a very great valley; and half of the mountain shall remove toward the north, and half of it toward the south. And ye shall flee to the valley of the mountains; for the valley of the mountains shall reach unto Azal; yea, ye shall flee, like as ye fled from before the earthquake in the days of Uzziah king of Judah: and the LORD my God shall come, and all the saints with thee. And it shall come to pass in that day, that the light shall not be clear, nor dark: But is shall be one day which shall be known to the LORD, not day, nor night: but it shall come to pass, that at evening time it shall be light. And it shall be in that day that living waters shall go out from Jerusalem; half of them toward the former sea, and half of them toward the hinder sea: in summer and in winter*

shall it be. And the LORD shall be king over all the earth: in that day shall there be one LORD, and his name one. All the land shall be turned as a plain from Geba to Rimmon south of Jerusalem: and it shall be lifted up, and inhabited in her place, from Benjamin's gate unto the place of the first gate, unto the corner gate, and from the tower of Hananeel unto the king's winepresses. And men shall dwell in it, and there shall be no more utter destruction; but Jerusalem shall be safely inhabited. And this shall be the plague wherewith the LORD will smite all the people that have fought against Jerusalem; Their flesh shall consume away while they stand upon their feet, and their eyes shall consume away in their holes, and their tongue shall consume away in their mouth. And it shall come to pass in that day, that a great tumult from the LORD shall be among them; and they shall lay hold every one on the hand of his neighbor, and his hand shall rise up against the hand of his neighbor. And Judah also shall fight at Jerusalem; and the wealth of all the heathen round about shall be gathered, gold and silver, and apparel, in great abundance. And so shall be the plague of the horse, of the mule, of the camel and of the ass, and of all the beasts that shall be in these tents, as this plague. And it shall come to pass, that every one that is left of all the nations which came against Jerusalem shall even go up from year to year to worship the King, the LORD of hosts, and to keep the feast of tabernacles. And it shall be, that whoso will not come up of all the families of the earth unto Jerusalem to worship the King, the LORD of hosts, even upon them shall be no rain. And if the family of Egypt go not up, and come not,

> *that have no rain; there shall be the plague, wherewith the LORD will smite the heathen that come not up to keep the feast of tabernacles. This shall be the punishment of Egypt, and the punishment of all nations that come not up to keep the feast of tabernacles. In that day shall there be upon the bells of the horses, HOLINESS UNTO THE LORD; and the pots in the LORD'S house shall be like the bowls before the altar. Yea, every pot in Jerusalem and in Judah shall be holiness unto the LORD of hosts: and all they that sacrifice shall come and take of them, and seethe therein: and in that day there shall be no more the Canaanite in the house of the LORD of hosts.*

- All nations will gather against Jerusalem to do battle.
- The LORD shall go forth and fight against all nations that come against Jerusalem.
- His feet will set down on the Mount of Olives. He will then destroy all the enemies of Israel.
- This will usher in the one thousand year reign of Jesus Christ over the world from the throne of Jerusalem.

Revelation 19:11-21:

> *And I saw heaven opened and behold a white horse; and he that sat upon him was called Faithful and True, and in righteousness he doth judge and make war. His eyes were as a flame of fire, and on his head were many crowns; and he had a name written, that no man knew, but he himself. And he was clothed with a vesture dipped in blood: and*

his name is called The Word of God. And the armies which were in heaven followed him upon white horses, clothed in fine linen, white and clean. And out of his mouth goeth a sharp sword, that with it he should smite the nations: and he shall rule them with a rod of iron: and he treadeth the winepress of the fierceness and wrath of Almighty God. And he hath on his vesture and on his thigh a name written, KING OF KINGS, AND LORD OF LORDS. And I saw an angel standing in the sun; and he cried with a loud voice, saying to all the fowls that fly in the midst of heaven, Come and gather yourselves together unto the supper of the great God. That ye may eat the flesh of kings, and the flesh of captains, and the flesh of mighty men, and the flesh of horses, and of them that sit on them, and the flesh of all men, both free and bond, both small and great. And I saw the beast, and the kings of the earth, and their armies, gathered together to make war against him that sat on the horse, and against his army. And the beast was taken, and with him the false prophet that wrought miracles before him, with which he deceived them that had received the mark of the beast, and them that worshipped his image. These both were cast alive into a lake of fire burning with brimstone. And the remnant were slain with the sword of him that sat upon the horse, which sword proceeded out of his mouth: and all the fowls were filled with their flesh.

This passage gives the prophecies of both Zechariah and Revelation understanding in recounting how the King will deliver Israel. This will be the establishment of God's rule of the world from the throne of Jerusalem.

Revelation 20:8-11

> *And shall go out to deceive the nations which are in the four quarters of the earth, Gog and Magog, to gather them together to battle: the number of whom is as the sand of the sea. And they went up on the breadth of the earth, and compassed the camp of the saints about, and the beloved city: and fire came down from God out of heaven, and devoured them. And the devil that deceived them was cast into the lake of fire and brimstone, where the beast and the false prophet are, and shall be tormented day and night forever and ever. And I saw a great white throne, and him that sat on it from whose face the earth and the heaven fled away; and there was found no place for them.*

Revelation is the account of these events where Gog and Magog attack Jerusalem. The God of Heaven will descend to the Earth and destroy the enemies of the Jews. This will liberate the city and initiate the one thousand year reign of Christ from Jerusalem.

In summary, these scriptures relate to us the turmoil to come. The accuracy of these accounts, taken together, demonstrates the true wonder of God's plan. Even though written thousands of years ago, their truths are as sure as God's promises to deliver His people.

Now I ask you two new questions:

- **Can you hear the rumbling horse's hooves making preparation to come against Israel?**
- **Can you now understand why the hatred of Israel is all a part of the plan of God?**

QUESTION # 15

What happens after Armageddon?

The exciting message is that the reign of the King of kings is coming! Finally, the proclaimed King will come to rule the world and He will accomplish that with a rod of iron.

The Christmas story tells us of the coming Prince of Peace. The rest of the story tells us how this Baby Prince grows up to become the King of the world. There are not many verses that clearly declare just how it will be during the reign of the King. We are told that He will rule the world from the throne of Jerusalem. Jesus came to the city of Jerusalem and proclaimed that after His death, He would rise from the dead. After He rose, He ascended into the heavens, confirmed by many who saw Him. The Old Testament prophets tell us the rest of the story. The writers of the rest of the New Testament also declared their expectations of His return and His rule. But Jesus' words told of things to come, and there are many scriptures that describe His return to this world.

He will then sit on the throne of David and rule with a rod of iron. This is only right, as Jesus, a Jew and of the lineage of David, will take His rightful place on the throne of David.

It is important to note that, after the death, burial, resurrection and ascension of the Lord Jesus Christ, (in 70 A.D.) the city of Jerusalem was destroyed. The walls, the temple, and the records in the temple were destroyed. The city was left in a pile of rubble. After the destruction of the city, the people of Israel were scattered all over the world, and were not restored until 1947. It was then that the United Nations declared their ability to regather and become a nation again. This is not coincidence: it was foretold. We must remember even today the Israelites do not have a king. Their figure of authority is the Prime Minister. In this part of the world, it is customary to have a king. But, when Israel became a nation, it chose for its political head to be called Prime Minister. What is the possible reason they did not choose a king? Perhaps Israel has finally come to understand and obey God's wishes. There is only one true king for Israel, and that title will be vacant until He, the only true King returns to rule Israel.

John 1:49 *"Nathaniel answered and saith unto him, Rabbi, thou art the Son of God; thou art the King of Israel."*

Matthew 21:5 *"Tell ye the daughter of Sion, Behold, thy king cometh unto thee, meek, and sitting upon an ass, and a colt the foal of an ass."*

Matthew 27:42 *"He saved others; himself he cannot save. If he be the King of Israel, let him now come down from the cross, and we will believe him."*

John 18:37 *"Pilate therefore said unto him, Art thou a king then?..."*

John 19:3 *"And said, Hail, King of the Jews!..."*

All these passages proclaim that the Jews were expecting their King, as did the Zechariah 14 passage several pages back.

The Prince of Peace, and His government are revealed in Isaiah 9:6-7, 61:10-11 and 62:11-12:

Isaiah 9:6-7 *"For unto us a child is born, unto us a son is given: and the government shall be upon his shoulder: and his name shall be called Wonderful, Counsellor, The mighty God, The everlasting Father, The Prince of Peace. Of the increase of his government and peace there shall be no end, upon the throne of David, and upon his kingdom to order it and to establish it with judgment and with justice from henceforth even for ever. The zeal of the LORD of hosts will perform this."*

Before all the nations, righteousness will spring forth.

Isaiah 61:10-11 *"I will greatly rejoice in the LORD, my soul shall be joyful in my God; for he hath clothed me with the garments of salvation, he hath covered me with the robe of righteousness, as a bridegroom decketh himself with ornaments, and as a bride adorneth herself with her jewels. For as the earth bringeth forth her bud, and as the garden causeth the things that are sown in it to spring forth; so the Lord God will cause righteousness and praise to spring forth before all the nations."*

The city of Jerusalem will finally be the city that all the world will rejoice in.

Isaiah 62:11-12 *"Behold, the LORD hath proclaimed unto the end of the world, Say ye to the daughter of Zion, Behold, thy salvation cometh; behold, his reward is with him, and his work before him. And they shall call them, The holy people, The redeemed of the LORD: and thou shalt be called, Sought out, A city not forsaken."*

The millennial kingdom will be the divine rule of the Earth. Christ will rule the world and He will not allow any disobedience. Jerusalem will be the center of His kingdom (Isaiah 2:1-4) and the disciples will reign with Christ (Matthew 19:28). Israel will be back in her land, sharing the glory of Christ, her rightful King. There will be total peace on the Earth between all of God's creation (Isaiah 11:7-9 and 54:13-14). There will be no waste in God's era; each man shall serve God to the best of his abilities. God's grace will be a wonderful thing to behold. There will still be human beings on Earth apart from the Church and the resurrected saints. The resurrected saints will exist in glorified bodies, ruling with Christ. There will still be children born to the humans who survived the seven years of trouble. They will be born into a sinful nature.

There will be, at the close of the millennium, many people who will have an outward appearance of commitment to the King, but deep down will harbor resentment for God because of His judgments or circumstances that they did not approve of while Jesus ruled them. Therefore, they will be given a chance to rebel by the unleashing of Satan back into the world. This will be at the very end of the thousand year reign of Christ. It is, however, important to note that this trial will be but a short time.

This brings us to question number sixteen.

QUESTION # 16

What then?

What of this event called "eternity?"

The Bible teaches that, after the thousand-year reign of King Jesus, Satan will be loosed for a time to test men and women who were born during the thousand-year period. Satan will gather anyone he can from the whole Earth to go up against King Jesus to do battle for the Earth and its future. God will then destroy Satan's army simply and quickly. This will usher in the White Throne Judgement and eternity. God will simply announce the battle is won and Satan has lost.

Revelation 20:11-15:

> *And I saw a great white throne, and him that sat on it, from whose face the earth and the heaven fled away; and there was found no place for them. And I saw the dead, small and great, stand before God; and the books were opened: and another book was opened, which is the book of life: and the dead were judged out of those things which were written in the books, according to their works. And the sea gave up the dead which were in it; and death and hell delivered up the dead which were in them: and they were judged every man according to their works. And death and hell were cast into the lake of fire. This is the second death. And whosoever*

was not found written in the book of life was cast into the lake of fire.

During the time of the great White Throne Judgment, those who were already dead and residing in Hell will be brought to stand before God. They will plead their case before the ultimate Judge of all creation. We know from other passages that the entering of one's name into the Lamb's Book of Life takes place when that one trusts the sacrifice of Jesus to make things right with God for him or her. The real issue is the Lamb's Book of Life. The only ones going into Heaven are those listed in the book.

When they are retrieved from Hell to plead their case and their name is not listed, they then are cast into the lake of fire for eternal punishment. It is after this event that God ushers in eternity. He begins by cleansing the Earth and somehow melting, purging, or even replacing the planet with a new one. We find this recorded in 2 Peter.

2 Peter 3:12-13 *"Looking for and hasting unto the coming of the day of God, wherein the heavens being on fire shall be dissolved, and the elements shall melt with fervent heat? Nevertheless we, according to his promise, look for new heavens and a new earth, wherein dwelleth righteousness."*

Revelation 21:1-2 *"And I saw a new heaven and a new earth: for the first heaven and the first earth were passed away; and there was no more sea. And I John saw the holy city, new Jerusalem, coming down from God out of heaven, prepared as a bride adorned for her husband."*

The New Jerusalem is a city that comes down from Heaven. This city is the place Jesus said He was going to build in John chapter 14. This city will come down and hover over the new Earth God has provided. This will usher in a new eternal state. God will Himself dwell with His people. Man and his Creator will be back to a face-to-face relationship. Just as Adam and Eve cast themselves out of God's favor, the blood of the Lamb will give man a new Garden of Eden to live again in God's favor. It was a long journey of separation and invited redemption, but for those who accept the invitation of Christ, a wonderful new personal relationship will be restored. How exciting!

The new Jerusalem and the new Earth are only part of eternity; there will be new heavens. Isaiah 66 gives us just a sneak preview of eternity and the wonderful relationship with the living God of Abraham. God, our Creator, has brought us full circle, just as in our life there is a beginning and an end. In God's plan there is a beginning (Abraham) and an end (Armageddon). But with salvation we can begin again. If Jesus decided to start His rule today, what kind of follower would you be? But even a better question is, would He find your name in the Lamb's Book of Life? Are you sure? Your eternity depends on it.

Isaiah 66:18-24:

> *For I know their works and their thoughts: it shall come, that I will gather all nations and tongues; and they shall come, and see my glory; And I will set a sign among them, and I will send those that escape of them unto the nations, to Tarshish, Pul, and Lud, that draw the bow, to Tubal, and Javan,*

> *to the isles afar off, that have not heard my fame, neither have seen my glory: and they shall declare my glory among the Gentiles. And they shall bring all your brethren for an offering unto the LORD out of all nations upon horses, and in chariots, and it litters, and upon mules, and upon swift beasts, to my holy mountain Jerusalem, saith the LORD, as the children of Israel bring an offering in a clean vessel into the house of the LORD. And I will also take of them for priests and for Levites, saith the LORD. For as the new heavens and the new earth, which I will make, shall remain before me, saith the LORD, so shall your seed and your name remain. And it shall come to pass, that from one new moon to another, and from one Sabbath to another, shall all flesh come to worship before me, saith the LORD. And they shall go forth, and look upon the carcases of the men that have transgressed against me: for their worm shall not die, neither shall their fire be quenched; and they shall be an abhorring unto all flesh.*

Notice those on Earth are traveling upward to worship God in the new Jerusalem. We are warned, however, that those who transgress against God will burn eternally.

Then comes the eternal life promised throughout the Bible to all those who are in a relationship with God.

Revelation 22:11-15:

> *He that is unjust, let him be unjust still: and he which is filthy, let him be filthy still: and he that is righteous, let him be righteous still: and he that is*

holy, let him be holy still. And, behold I come quickly; and my reward is with me, to give every man according as his work shall be. I am Alpha and Omega, the beginning and the end, the first and the last. Blessed are they that do his commandments, that they may have right to the tree of life, and may enter in through the gates into the city. For without are dogs, and sorcerers, and whoremongers, and murderers, and idolators, and whosoever loveth and maketh a lie.

Revelation 22 – The eternal existence

Revelation 22 states some very hard but welcome facts:

1. Eternity is just that – eternal!
2. The things that were settled before are settled forever – it's final.
3. Those outside will not have a chance to ever be inside.
   - **Is there a God?**
   - **If so, does He have a reason for creating the people called the Jews?**
   - **Is He manipulating the events of the world to serve His purpose?**
   - **To what extent has He already determined what has taken place and will take place in this world?**

These are cold but bold truths declared to us. Just as God's unfolding story is coming to a close, so must our study of Abraham to Armageddon. But it is not too late to ensure your place in eternity. How do we do that? I'm glad you asked. Let's move to the conclusion and try to help all come to know, so we will not be outside of God's presence any more, ever.

CONCLUSION

How this applies to us

1. The Sacrificial System Established!

   When the sons of Adam and Eve realized what they were missing outside the Garden of Eden and that they separated themselves from God, they began to search for ways to be able to get back into good standing with their Creator. They struggled over the answer. Cain tried to please God with what he had labored to produce, but God rejected his efforts. Abel then killed a lamb and presented it to God for His approval. God received his efforts and was pleased with Abel. This, in turn, brought division between the two brothers. This division ended in a war that cost Abel his life and Cain his future. However, this encounter stands as the introduction to the way to become reinstated into good standing with the Creator. There is only one way – there must be a blood sacrifice and death must come by way of this sacrifice. It must be an innocent, pure sacrifice such as a lamb, pigeon, dove, etc. Thus began the teaching of the sacrificial system. This continued up to Abraham, as he was asked by God to give his promised son as a sacrifice to show his love for God. Abraham was so in love with and had such trust in God that he was willing, and went to the mountain to sacrifice his own son. But God stopped him, and instead gave Abraham a sacrifice to take the place of Isaac, who was about to die to proclaim Abraham's love for and trust in God. Instead, God would provide His Son to show His love for mankind. Abraham looked up and saw a ram with its head caught in a thicket. Abraham sacrificed this ram instead of his son. This is a direct connection to Jesus Christ, the Son of God, who was found standing in the temple and on the same place where Abraham found the ram in the thicket. Christ wore the symbol of the thicket in a crown of thorns on His head. The words of Abraham in Genesis 22:8 *"...God will provide Himself a lamb for a burnt offering,"* came boldly true. The death of Christ fulfilled the proclamation. Jesus was the Lamb of Abel, and Jesus was the Lamb of Abraham. He (Jesus) came and was sacrificed for the sins of the world – both Jews and Gentiles alike. He is the Lamb that the world needed in order to return to the grace of God. What God asks of us is much easier than what He asked of Abraham. We need not sacrifice a loved one, or for that matter, even an animal. We must only sacrifice our pride and self, acknowledging Christ as our Savior and Lord. God sacrificed something dear to Himself to prove His love for us. This gives new meaning to the very well-known verse, John 3:16 *"For God so loved the world, that He gave His only begotten Son, that whosoever believeth in him should not perish, but have everlasting life."*

There are other very powerful passages that reach out to us through the pages of the Bible pointing to the coming of the Sacrifice to redeem mankind. One of the greatest is Isaiah 53:-1-12:

Who hath believed our report? And to whom is the arm of the LORD revealed? For he shall grow up before him as a tender plant, and as a root out of a dry ground: he hath no form nor comeliness; and when we shall see him, there is no beauty that we should desire him. He is despised and rejected of men: a man of sorrows, and acquainted with grief: and we hid as it were our faces from him; he was despised, and we esteemed him not. Surely he hath borne our griefs, and carried our sorrows: yet we did esteem him stricken, smitten of God, and afflicted. But he was wounded for our transgressions, he was bruised for our iniquities: the chastisement of our peace was upon him; and with his stripes we are healed. All we like sheep have gone astray; we have turned every one to his own way; and the LORD hath laid on him the iniquity of us all. He was oppressed, and he was afflicted, yet he opened not his mouth: he is brought as a lamb to the slaughter, and as a sheep before her shearers is dumb, so he opened not his mouth. He was taken from prison and from judgment: and who shall declare his generation? For he was cut off out of the land of the living: for the transgression of my people was he stricken. And he made his grave with the wicked, and with the rich in his death; because he had done no violence, neither was any deceit in his mouth. Yet it pleased the LORD to bruise him: he hath put him to grief: when thou shalt make his soul an offering for sin, he shall see his seed, he shall prolong his days, and the pleasure of the LORD

> *shall prosper in his hand. He shall see of the travail of his soul, and shall be satisfied: by his knowledge shall my righteous servant justify many; for he shall bear their iniquities. Therefore will I divide him a portion with the great, and he shall divide the spoil with the strong; because he hath poured out his soul unto death: and he was numbered with the transgressors; and he bare the sin of many, and made intercession for the transgressors.*

The wonder of God's plan is His creation of the people called Jews. God created a sacrificial system that would be accepted as the way to please God. He then sent His Son to be that sacrifice. He subsequently sent His Church to the rest of the world to proclaim the sacrificial work of Jesus to make us right with our Creator.

One might ask, "How can the rest of the world understand this?" The rest of the world has sacrificial systems in place. All mankind understands the teaching of sacrifice. Every society, whatever the time frame, understands the teaching of sacrifice. However, the rest of the world has polluted or distorted the system. Some have even used sacrifice to satisfy their dead gods. Notice however, that they are doing the sacrificing. Just as Abraham was called on by God to sacrifice His most precious possession, God stepped in and would not allow it. The other dead gods do not step in and stop it because they are dead. But the Creator is very much alive and has stepped in and sacrificed so we would not need to do so.

2. The Law Declared Righteousness!

Before Moses, there was an unwritten teaching of right and wrong, but nothing definite. Mankind was simply running on the words of his forefathers and becoming more corrupt with each generation. God even had to step in and wipe out almost every part of His creation with the flood to restart mankind. Therefore, God created and called the children of Abraham to establish His law. They did not know what God was doing, but they ended up in Egypt, enlarged in their population, but oppressed in their lifestyle. The fact is, they were in bondage and slavery, so God sent Moses to deliver them. They were delivered by God's powerful hand and then Moses began to put down in writing the story of man's beginning as well as the expectations of man's Creator. We refer to it as the Law of God. This Law declared just that – God's expectation for man, which is righteousness. The Law was so rigid that man could not keep it even though he tried. And then God sent His Son to bring grace. Grace gave us the way to become a part of God's Son, and in turn, stand in His righteousness and not our own. By the Law of Moses, man learned what is righteous. When the Son of God came into this world and lived righteously, mankind realized that Jesus must be God in order to have lived the whole Law. When Jesus stood before the priests of the Jerusalem temple, as the proclaimed King of the Jews, Pilate of the Romans and Herod found Him righteous. The only reason they killed Him was because He said that He was God (I Am). Even this was the truth. The point is, we, through the Jews, now know the absolute truth.

3. Eternity Declared: Life or Death!

By and through the story of the Jews, mankind discovered that there is life after death for all humanity. It is very apparent that death exists. We see it every day. It is a fact that cannot be denied. We can pick up any newspaper and read about the people who died today. But why do we die? Why do we bury people in the ground? What is on the other side of death? The answers to these questions are found in the Bible. The Jewish scribes preserved the writings of Moses and the prophets to explain these things to us. Many books have arrived on the scene today that try to answer the many questions about death. There is only one book that answers the call of death and gives it meaning. That book, which was written miraculously, is obviously the greatest story ever told,. The Bible was penned by over 40 writers in three different languages, on three continents, over a time span of nearly 4,000 years, and is compiled of 66 different books. But it still fits together like a fine-tuned watch. The Bible defines death as separation from God. When Adam and Eve disobeyed God, they were never able to go into the presence of God again. They died to the audience of God. They found themselves unrighteous and unwelcome in God's house. Therefore, they could not exist in His holy presence. But we must understand that the Bible teaches that the soul of man will always exist. God created man and breathed into him a living soul. The

Bible goes on to declare that if a person does not become in good standing with God by the sacrifice of lambs (and eventually the Lamb Jesus), they will be cast away from God into a place of torment called Hell or the abode of the dead. It (the Bible) declares that there will be torture of fire there.

Eternity exists for everyone. But for the lost (unrepentant, unrighteous, unjustified, Cainites) there is eternal judgment and eternal punishment. For the ones found righteous by standing with faith in the Lamb's work (Jesus), there is peace, rest, and eternal blessing – they have become Abelites.

I'm sure by now you know the answer to the question regarding God's existence. It is a resounding, bold "YES!" **God does exist, and He does have a reason for creating a people called the Jews. Furthermore, He is manipulating the events of the world to serve His purposes.**

This is the author's answer, but now you must answer these questions for yourself.

SUMMARY, COMFORT AND RESPONSE

Summary

Isaiah 62:11-12 *"Behold, the LORD hath proclaimed unto the end of the world, Say ye to the daughter of Zion, Behold thy salvation cometh; behold, his reward is with him, and his work before him. And they shall call them, The holy people, The redeemed of the LORD: and thou shalt be called, Sought out. A city not forsaken."*

- God's chosen people – a billboard and clock to the rest of the world
- God's chosen people – examples of what righteousness is (the Law of Moses)
- God's chosen people – examples of God's judgment on unrighteousness

GOD'S PLAN FOR REACHING THE REST OF THE WORLD

- God's chosen people rejected God's calling on them – therefore God turned to the rest of the world
- God's plan to reach the world through what He called His Church
- God's chosen people regathered to be used to focus the world's attention on the truth of the Bible
- God's chosen people hated once again, therefore drawing attention to the Word of God.
- God's chosen people – efforts to reach them during Revelation chapters 4-17
- Armageddon and the rule of iron
- Eternal judgments and eternity

Comfort

Take comfort in the fact that God is good, caring, righteous, full of mercy and grace, and desires to call us to Himself. We can take comfort in the fact that God is the One in charge of this world, and no one else. We must take comfort in the fact that this world is not just spinning on its own without a good God looking on to take care of the end results.

It has been said that we Christians simply need a crutch to make us feel that some great God is looking out for us. But we should not be ashamed to admit that we need God's help. There can be no better crutch than God to lean on. The crutch that God has chosen to use is the wooden crutch called the cross. To those who argue, I have an answer. The world has turned on itself, and is close to destruction. Would you wish to lean on yourself, your friends, or the Christ and the cross He has provided?

We need someone to look out for us, and those who would say differently are lying to themselves. But I am very glad to find that the facts do point to a good God truly in control of the world's destiny. It is even better news that He sent His Son to prove His love toward us. He wants a Father/child relationship with us. It is wonderful that the facts tell us that we can trust Him for our well-being today, tomorrow and for eternity. Take comfort in these words.

The nation of Israel has played out a drama that tells interested parties that God is a Rewarder of those who diligently seek Him. I ask, is that you? You may be telling yourself, "I have time, since many events are still to come." The uncertainty of life makes that a dangerous proposition. If you tragically lost your life tomorrow, where would you be in God's plan? Is He ready to write your name in the Book of Life? There is no time to wait. There are those who believed they had time, and now they remain dead with only the future promise of eternal damnation. I ask you to make the choice to join those living for eternity.

Response

I hope this book has brought you some comfort in God's future plan for this world. Now you know the problem of man is that we are alienated from God by our sin. We are incomplete without Him. He has gone to great lengths to help us recognize these important truths. Now we know that Jesus was sent into the world to redeem us out of our alienated state and into the kingdom, the Church, and into a relationship with the Creator and Controller of all the elements of this world. Will you know all these things and do nothing? Or will you call upon this God through the Lamb that was slain? If so, pray this prayer right now:

Dear Father, I recognize that I am a sinner. I confess that I need You to forgive me of my sinful rebellion. I recognize that without the cleansing of the blood of Jesus, I will continue to be separated from You, and I do not want that. Please take the blood that Jesus shed for me, and wash me clean with it. I plead the blood of Jesus Christ, the Lamb that was slain. I repent and turn from my sinfulness to follow your Lordship now. I claim Jesus as my one and only LORD and KING. Jesus, thank You for dying for me. Thank You for offering forgiveness to me, and thank You for saving my soul from eternal separation from God. I claim the promises of the Word of God. John 6:37 – 'him that cometh to me I will in no wise cast out." Romans 10:9 – "if thou shalt confess with thy mouth the Lord Jesus, and shalt believe in thine heart that God hath raised him from the dead, thou shalt be saved." I have called, I confess, and I believe! Thank You, Lord, for forgiving, saving and receiving me!

Now you are a born-again Christian! Now you are to work for Him and help others come to understand what you know. Peter called you a royal priest (1 Peter 2:9). I encourage you now to go and find a Bible-preaching Church, ask about being baptized, and link up with one of God's Churches to work from and to grow in.

I would also encourage you to find those nonbelievers, take a copy of this book, and compel them to read it, so that God may speak to them. This book was written to answer questions about God: whether He exists, and if so, what His plan is and how you can connect with Him. Go into your world and proclaim. But remember, the world will not care how much you know until they know how much you care. Your life speaks louder than words. Go!

Footnotes

1. Clarence Larken, "Dispensational Truth or God's Plan and Purposes in the Ages" published by Clarence Larken Foundation, 1918, pages 159-161.
2. ErGun Mehmet Caner and Emir Fethi Caner, "Unveiling Islam" published by Kregel Publications, 2002, pages 30-32.

References

Unveiling Islam, by Ergun Mehmet Caner and Emir Fethi Caner, published by Kregel, Grand Rapids, MI, Copyrighted 2002

Islam Revealed (A Christian Arab's View of Islam), by Dr. Anis A. Shorrosh, published by Thomas Nelson, Nashville, TN, Copyrighted 1988

The Seven Festivals of the Messiah, by Edward Chumney, published by Destiny Image, Inc., Shippensburg, PA, Cpyrighted 1994

Dispensational Truths or God's Plan and Purposes in the Ages, by Clarence Larken, published by Clarence Larkin Foundation, Copyrighted 1918

The American Educator Encyclopedia, B.S. University of Illinois; Drake U., Loyola U., American Conservatory, published by The United Educators, Inc. Publishers, Lake Bluff, IL, Copyrighted 1967

Encyclopedia Dictionary of Judaica, published by Keter Publishing House, Jerusalem, Israel, Edicted by Geoffrey Wigoder

Jerusalmen Chronicles New of the Past, A Publication of the Reubeni Foundation, Jerusalem Editor-in-Chief, Volume One: The Dawn of Redemption, Volume Two: The Rise of Christianity, Volume Three: In the Days of the Bible

The Day Israel Dies! By Salem Kirban, published by Salem Kirban, Huntingdon Valley, PA

Https://www.museumoftolerance.com/education/teacher-resources/holocaust-resources/36-questions-about-the-holocaust.html#1

www.ingramcontent.com/pod-product-compliance
Lightning Source LLC
Chambersburg PA
CBHW030521080526
44586CB00011B/277